Your Child's Emotional Health: The Middle Years

Philadelphia Child Guidance Center

Your Child's Emotional Health: The Middle Years

**PHILADELPHIA
CHILD GUIDANCE CENTER
WITH JACK MAGUIRE**

Produced by The Philip Lief Group, Inc.

Macmillan • USA

This book is not intended as a substitute for the professional advice of a doctor or mental health professional. The reader should regularly consult a physician or appropriate health care practitioner in matters relating to health, particularly with respect to any symptoms that may require diagnosis or medical attention.

MACMILLAN
A Prentice Hall Macmillan Company
15 Columbus Circle
New York, NY 10023

Published by arrangement with   The Philip Lief Group, Inc.
                                6 West 20th Street
                                New York, NY 10011

MACMILLAN is a registered trademark of Macmillan, Inc.

Library of Congress Cataloging-in-Publication Data

Your child's emotional health. The middle years / Philadelphia Child Guidance Center with Jack Maguire.
    p.   cm.
  Includes index.
  ISBN 0-02-860002-9
  1. Emotions in children. 2. Emotional problems of children. I. Maguire, Jack. II. Philadelphia Child Guidance Center.
BF723.E6Y69   1995
649'.124—dc20   94-34152
                                                          CIP

Manufactured in the United States of America

10 9 8 7 6 5 4 3 2 1

This book is dedicated to Margie Ouellette
and to her children,
Amanda, Carly, and Brittany.
I am proud to be a part of their family.

Contents

Preface

C hildren seldom say that they need help. More often their behaviors tell us that they do. They may suffer vague, slowly evolving difficulties at home, at school, or with their peers. Or they may exhibit sudden, marked changes in their conduct and mood that pervade every aspect of their lives.

Each year, thousands of children, adolescents, and their families get help from Philadelphia Child Guidance Center (PCGC). As one of the foremost centers in the country for child and adolescent psychiatric care, PCGC offers services that are specialized and individually designed to meet the needs of each child and family. Often working in closely cooperative teams, staff members help families recognize, expand, and mobilize their strengths to make life more fulfilling for the affected child as well as for the family as a whole.

Since PCGC's origin in 1925 as one of the first centers in the world devoted to child psychiatry, it has enjoyed an international reputation for its excellent treatment and innovative research. The founding director, Frederick H. Allen, M.D., was the first board-certified child psychiatrist in the United States as well as one of the first psychiatrists to address the problems of the child in the context of the family. Within his historic thirty-year tenure, PCGC achieved a leadership position in the study and treatment of emotional problems affecting children from birth through adolescence.

Later, under the auspices of Director Salvador Minuchin, M.D., PCGC pioneered the development of structural family therapy, a systems-oriented approach that views diagnosis and treatment of a child in the context of the family and social relationships in which she or he lives. Included in that context are the child's extended family, friends, caretakers, school, and all agencies in the culture at large— social, legal, religious, recreational, and health oriented—that influence the child's life.

Today, under the clinical direction of Alberto C. Serrano, M.D., PCGC's staff of 230 professionals provides a broad range of diagnostic and therapeutic programs that directly benefit the mid-Atlantic region of the United States and serve as models for other diagnostic and therapeutic programs throughout the nation and abroad. Thanks to its strong affiliation with the University of Pennsylvania Medical School, The Children's Hospital of Philadelphia, and Children's Seashore House, PCGC is a major component of one of the most advanced health-care and health-care research centers in the country.

This books draws upon the unique experience and expertise of PCGC to offer you, as parents, practical guidelines for raising your child to be emotionally healthy. Specifically, it helps you perform the following, especially challenging activities:

■ identify and assess your child's emotional states, problems, capabilities, and needs;

■ develop an effective parenting style that best suits you and your child as individuals;

■ address the most common and most troublesome emotional difficulties that can arise in the course of your child's life;

■ ensure the emotional well-being of all family members during any emotional crisis experienced by your family as a whole or by your child individually;

■ determine if and when you, your family, and your child need professional help in managing emotional difficulties;

■ secure the professional help that is most appropriate for you, your family, and your child, according to the situation at hand.

Love for a child comes naturally to a parent and can go far toward giving a child emotional security. Parenting skills, however, are also required to meet a child's emotional needs, and they do *not* come naturally. Instead, parents must learn them.

This book is specially designed to help parents help themselves so that they in turn can help their children. Underlying everything that PCGC does—and represents—is the belief that family members have the ability to work together to solve their problems and that each family member can achieve a new and more rewarding life in the process.

Acknowledgments

A mong the many people outside Philadelphia Child Guidance Center who were helpful in putting this book together, I'd like to give special thanks to Eva Weiss, to The Philip Lief Group as a whole, and to Natalie Chapman, my editor at Macmillan. Their "writer guidance" was invaluable.

Your
Child's
Emotional
Health:
The Middle
Years

Introduction

The transition from being a preschool child to being a school-age child can be likened to that amphibious period in evolutionary history when animals first began living on land as well as in water. From age six to age thirteen, human beings live in a privileged middle phase between babyhood, when they are physically and intellectually underdeveloped and completely dependent on their parents, and puberty, when they so dramatically enter the final stage of their maturing process and their dependence on their parents.

From a child's perspective, the middle period of childhood is an especially glorious time of first discovering all the wonders of kinship, friendship, education, and life itself. However, the middle years are also especially vulnerable ones, filled with all sorts of intimidating new duties and challenges.

A child in the middle years is forced to engage in a balancing act she or he didn't have to perform during the early years. Within the family, the child at this stage of life is expected to assume more and more responsibility for doing chores, for meeting her or his personal needs, and for managing many of her or his interpersonal problems with siblings and other relatives. At school, the child is faced with the task of developing more and more proficiency in numerous, different academic areas. Among peers, the child must play increasingly more sophisticated social games in order to achieve and retain popularity and self-esteem.

All the while that a child during the middle years is compelled to perform this balancing act, she or he is also coming to terms with the beauties and terrors of society at large. If personal experiences of the outside world don't expose a child to poverty, crime, violence, injustice, or catastrophe, then television will. The result of such exposure can, at times, be emotionally devastating. And there's always the frightening possibility that the child will fall victim to the worst ills of the outside world by running away or experimenting with drugs or alcohol or having dangerous sexual encounters.

Nevertheless, the middle years of childhood in most cases constitute the golden age of childhood, an era of emotional awakening, growth, and engagement that is exciting in itself and lays the foundation for a rich and rewarding life as an adult. To help ensure your child's emotional well-being throughout this period, keep in mind these basic truths:

1. The maintenance of a good ongoing dialogue between parent and child during the middle years is vital to the latter's emotional health.

A school-age child is intensely involved in developing verbal communication skills; they should be tapped to enhance the quality of the parent-child relationship. Make it easy and comfortable for your child to express experiences and feelings to you by initiating conversations with her or him on a frequent, regular, and dependable basis. Be an active listener whenever your child is speaking to you and withhold judgment about what is communicated whenever possible.

Conversations with your children are your single best source of information about their emotional state of being and the factors contributing to it. But perhaps even more important, these conversations help them put experiences and feelings into perspective so that they can be appreciated more fully and constructively.

2. A child in the middle years needs to be granted a certain amount of independence, even if it entails a certain amount of risk.

However much you may want to protect your school-age child from any physical, emotional, or social harm, you need to allow your child some freedom to discover her or his capabilities and limitations and to learn from mistakes and misfortunes. The more carefully—and discreetly—you observe your child and the more effectively you consult with other knowledgeable people about your child, the better equipped you will be to make difficult decisions regarding how much independence to grant her or him in specific situations.

3. A child in the middle years thrives on praise and support.

A school-age child is constantly being critiqued for shortcomings in school, games, friendships, personal conduct, and chore performance. This barrage of criticism needs to be offset by sincere and hearty praise whenever it's appropriate. Your child also needs to be confident that you will always be there if your help is needed or requested.

The material presented in this section of the book will assist you in maintaining an emotionally supportive and helpful relationship with your school-age child. It is organized as follows:

- timetable of major stress issues during the middle years

- guidelines for evaluating the existence and extent of depression or stress in a school-age child's life

- how to help a child cope with a family move

- how to help a child cope with serious illness

- at PCGC: seasonal affective disorder

- at PCGC: pain management for school-age children

7. LYING AND STEALING *(Page 76)*

- the causes and effects of lying and stealing in the life of a school-age child

- how to cope with lying and stealing when it happens

8. SIBLING RIVALRY *(Page 80)*

- how and why sibling rivalry develops

- how to prevent and manage sibling rivalry

9. DIVORCE *(Page 85)*

- how to announce and explain a divorce to school-age children

- how to help a school-age child cope emotionally with a divorce while it's in progress

- how to help a school-age child cope emotionally with parental dating and remarriage

10. THE ADOPTED CHILD *(Page 91)*

- the causes and effects of common emotional problems associated with being an adopted child

- how to talk with a school-age child about her or his adopted status

- how to help a school-age child cope with adoption-related emotional problems

11. SCHOOL *(Page 96)*

- the causes and effects of common emotional problems associated with school life

■ how to help your child avoid or cope with school-related emotional problems

■ guidelines for evaluating whether or not it may be beneficial for a school-age child's emotional health to repeat or skip a grade

12. FRIENDSHIP *(Page 102)*

■ common problems associated with a school-age child's friendships and how to cope with these problems

■ guidelines for evaluating whether a school-age child may be overly shy or aggressive

■ how bully-victim relationships develop and how to help potential bullies or potential victims avoid, or defuse, such relationships

13. TELEVISION *(Page 112)*

■ the positive and negative emotional effects of television viewing on school-age children

■ how to manage your child's television viewing so that it doesn't interfere with her or his emotional well-being

14. PSYCHOTHERAPY *(Page 116)*

■ how to determine if your school-age child might need psychotherapy

■ how to choose the appropriate therapy and a doctor/therapist

■ the meaning behind special diagnoses: attention-deficit hyperactivity disorder and learning disabilities

■ at PCGC: ADHD evaluation and treatment

The Middle Years:
An Emotional Time Line

Although it's difficult to define what is "normal" in the year-to-year emotional life of a school-age child, here are some very broad guidelines:

SIX TO SEVEN YEARS

■ tends to exhibit extremes of emotional responses: for example, exuberant delight instead of a quiet joy or hysterical crying instead of simple sadness

■ is very susceptible to having hurt feelings

■ may exhibit "school phobia," a fear of going to school that can lead to feigned or psychosomatic illness

■ quarrels with parents—especially mother—as a means of discharging separation anxiety associated with starting school life or of testing parent-child relationship in this new school-oriented stage of life

■ forms multiple, relatively superficial, and relatively short-lasting relationships with peers

■ engages in "sex play" to satisfy curiosity about genitals

■ frequently initiates sibling rivalry

■ occasionally resorts to lying or stealing as a coping mechanism or a means of rebellion

SEVEN TO NINE YEARS

■ exhibits much more emotional equilibrium than previously, although at age eight may go through a recurrence of extreme emotional reactions and quarrels with parents

■ experiences both fear and rational concern related to possible dangers lurking in the outside world: crime, violence, catastrophe

■ becomes interested in sex talk and sex jokes and is curious about the mechanics of reproduction

■ develops crushes on peers

■ handles competitive play—and losing—pretty well

■ worries about failure in academic performance

■ assumes more responsibility for own acts instead of blaming others

■ fears being wrong or being humiliated

NINE TO ELEVEN YEARS

■ is generally happy and content

■ relies more and more on peers as opposed to parents for evaluation, approval, and direction

■ forms "puppy love" relationships with peers

■ develops much more mature relationships with siblings

■ exhibits concern over issues of justness and fairness

■ seeks and develops a "best friend" relationship

■ worries about the possibility of parents' fighting, divorcing, losing their jobs, becoming ill, or dying

ELEVEN TO THIRTEEN YEARS (EARLY ADOLESCENCE)

■ becomes very self-conscious and sensitive about physical development, physical health, and sexuality

■ fears losing possessions, popularity, or status

■ develops more and more romantic attachments with peers

■ occasionally loses patience with siblings and parents as they increasingly interfere with personal, peer-related interactions and ambitions

■ seeks and develops a close circle of friends for social support

■ frequently exhibits moodiness and irritability

Psychosomatic Illness

By definition, a psychosomatic illness is a genuine physical illness that has psychological, as well as biological, causes (*psycho*: the Greek root for mind; *soma*: the Greek root for body). More technically, such an illness is known as a *psychophysiological disorder*. As a rule, when the underlying physiological problem is effectively addressed, the physical symptoms of the illness are greatly alleviated and may even disappear.

The body and the mind are so interconnected that almost any illness can be said to have a psychosomatic component. However, certain stress-sensitive illnesses are commonly thought to be especially psychosomatic in nature, such as ulcers, headaches, stomachaches, asthma, high blood pressure, skin rashes or blemishes, and allergies.

Several factors besides exposure to stress increase the tendency of a child to suffer from illnesses that are especially psychosomatic in nature. One factor involves the "built-in" reactivity of the child's nervous system. Some individuals are born with nervous systems that produce strong responses to outside stimuli; some are not. The "high reactors" experience stronger responses to outside stimuli, which can make them basically shy (an unconscious defense against possible stress) as well as predispose them toward psychosomatic illnesses.

Another factor predisposing a child to psychosomatic illness can be the vulnerability of a particular organ or system in the child's body. Due to heredity or a prior illness, a child may have impaired lungs, a quirky digestive system, or any number of physiological weaknesses that render her or him more susceptible to stress-related physical problems.

Finally, a major factor affecting psychosomatic reactions in children during the middle years involves what they are taught—directly or indirectly—about the connection between stress and illness in particular and emotional health and physical health in general. A school-age child's mental/emotional life interacts with her or his physiological life very closely— much more closely than adults can usually appreciate.

For example, a child who receives loving attention only when not feeling well can eventually "learn" how to be sick more easily and more often. So can the child who is automatically allowed to stay home from school whenever she or he doesn't feel well and the child who is prompted to fear certain physical illnesses without being given sufficient understanding of them or practical guidance on how to avoid or manage them.

Alternatively, a child who regularly experiences caring and comforting love, whether healthy or ill, is less likely to respond to occasional neglect with illness. A child who is always encouraged to communicate openly about physical and emotional feelings, knowing that her or his parents are concerned about these feelings, is less likely to express displeasure with school—or with anything else—through physical symptoms. And a child who receives an ongoing, commonsense education about stress triggers and physical illnesses is better equipped to avoid or manage them.

Cognitive Development

Separate from, but interrelated with, a child's emotional development is her or his cognitive development. The expression "cognitive development" refers to a child's ability to perceive, think, and remember. As such, it is more closely associated with intellectual capabilities than with psychological makeup.

How a child feels is bound to affect how she or he perceives, thinks, and remembers—and vice versa. However, the particular cause-and-effect relationship between a child's cognitive and emotional development depends on biological and social variables and differs greatly from individual to individual. Therefore, any useful picture of such a relationship in the case of a specific child can only be drawn in the context of comprehensive therapeutic treatment.

Among the many theories concerning cognitive development in children, that of the French psychologist Jean Piaget is the most popular. It divides a child's cognitive development during the early years into two distinct, age-related stages that can be described as follows:

1. Sensory-motor thinking

This stage is associated with infancy. The child acquires the ability to identify and remember different facets of the physical world (e.g., faces, sounds, toys, smells, foods). The child also learns to connect certain perceptions with certain physical actions (e.g., judging distances, moving within a given set of physical parameters, anticipating the course of simple gestures and events).

2. Intuitive and representational thinking

This stage is associated with toddlers and preschoolers. The child acquires language skills, recognizes major differences in individual points of view, formulates simple stories, ideas, or plans, and develops an understanding of basic time-and-space concepts.

During the middle years (ages six to thirteen), a child goes through the *concrete operations* stage of cognitive development, during which she or he develops logic and the ability to perform core intellectual activities, for example, reading, writing, computing, and experimenting. Thereafter—that is, through ado-

lescence and adulthood—an individual is involved in the
formal operations stage of cognitive development, during
which she or he refines intellectual capabilities and learns to
conceptualize more and more philosophically.

At PCGC:
Psychological Testing in
the Middle Years

Mental-health professionals, physicians, school personnel, and
other specialists frequently make decisions that have a profound influence on children during their middle years. His-
torically, psychological testing has been a widely used and
valued method for providing such professionals with the proper
information to make those decisions.

Psychological testing is generally employed to determine
individual differences and needs by providing specifics about
a school-age child's abilities, strengths, personality style, and
emotional functioning. It is also helpful in evaluating the actual or potential effects on school-age children of significant
situational events, such as moving to a new home, coping with
a serious illness, or going through a parental divorce.

For children between the ages of six and thirteen, psychological testing provides data about intellectual capacities,
problem-solving strategies, neuropsychological processing,
and personality styles. In addition, academic achievement is
tested in order to assess the possible presence of learning disorders. Tests that PCGC frequently recommends or uses for
personality analysis include the Rorschach test (recently re-
juvenated and rendered more useful by a research-based scor-
ing system), the Thematic Apperception Test, and Sentence
Completion Tests.

The experience of PCGC has shown that the more the family
is informed about the testing and involved in the testing process, the more useful the evaluation is to them. Therefore,
PCGC employs and advocates the following testing process:

■ The first step in the process is to help the child understand
the purpose of the testing. For example, it is counterproductive

to tell six- or seven-year-old children that they are "going to play some games." Instead, they should be told, in a manner that they can understand and appreciate, that they are going to find out how best their minds work so that family and school situations can be made better for them.

■ Before the testing itself begins, the psychologist or test administrator meets with the child and parents to identify the reasons why testing is being sought, obtain relevant background history, address any initial questions or concerns the child and parents have, and explain the testing process.

■ It helps to have between two and four short, separate testing sessions rather than one long one. That way, fatigue factors are minimized, and a fuller range of the child's accomplishments and capabilities can be tested.

■ When testing is completed, the results are discussed with the family and the child.

For more information about psychological testing of school-age children, consult your physician, school counselor, or a local mental-health agency.

1.

Sexuality

Sigmund Freud referred to the years between age six and age eleven as the "latency period." He believed that a child within this age range is relatively unconcerned with sexual matters and that any such interest is much more likely to be motivated by scientific curiosity than by romantic or erotic feelings.

Today experts debate about whether Freud was accurate in describing this age span as sexually "latent." Nevertheless, it certainly *appears* that a child's sexuality causes much less emotional turmoil during the middle years than it does in the years immediately before and after.

From approximately age four to age six, when children are first becoming consciously aware of sexual roles and sexual activities, they typically endure an intense romantic attraction to their parent of the opposite sex (or, in the absence of this parent, to some other adult of the opposite sex who plays a major role in their life). In response to this powerful attraction, they also experience a strong feeling of competitiveness and even anger focused on the parent of the same sex (or toward anyone romantically interested in their love object).

In the case of boys, Freud called this phenomenon an Oedipus complex, after the legendary Greek hero and supposed orphan who unknowingly killed his father and married his mother. In the case of girls, he called it an Electra complex, after the daughter of the Greek King Agamemnon, who killed her mother out of love for her father.

Whatever modern experts may label this phenomenon, most of them agree with Freud that it's a growth experience characterized by great emotional upheaval. They also agree that the middle years represent a stabilizing recovery period, during which children form more rational and practical partnerships with their parents and other adults they love. The more effectively parents learn to manage sex-related issues associated with the middle years, the better these partnerships develop.

At the other extreme from the middle years is adolescence. The very word suggests an era of newly emerging sexuality, at frequent and dramatic odds with the individual's ongoing family dependence, social immaturity, and personal lack of self-confidence.

Compared to the average teenager's life, the average school-age kid's life is decidedly more peaceful in terms of sex-related matters. But how much turmoil individual children actually experience when they are teenagers depends to a great extent on how successfully their parents prepare them for adolescence during their middle years.

In issues having to do with a school-age child's sexuality, your major contribution will be educational. As an educator, your biggest challenge will be discussing the emotions and ethics that are associated with sexuality. It's not an easy task by any means, but it's an essential one if your child is to mature into a healthy, satisfied, and morally decent adult.

When you converse with your child about the emotions and ethics associated with sex, you have little choice but to let your conscience be your guide and hope for the best. Awkward though it may be to describe to your child the mechanics of sexual intercourse, menstruation, conception, pregnancy, and birth, at least you can speak with a more or less scientific detachment. When it comes to talking with your child about sexual feelings and responsibilities, you must speak from your heart. Only through a very sensitive and compassionate dialogue can you communicate to your child how to exercise safety, self-control, and regard for others in sexual situations—and why.

Take advantage of every opportunity that your school-age child gives you to talk about sexuality; in these discussions, always try to interrelate the mechanical aspects of sex with its emotional and ethical aspects. Also, be alert for signs that your child may require such a talk, even though she or he may not be forthcoming about the need. Possible signs of this nature include making flip or erroneous statements about sex, introducing sexual content into solitary or group play, and expressing noticeable interest in sex-related songs, television programs, or printed matter.

Here are some additional tips for discussing, and dealing with, your school-age child's sexuality:

■ *Discuss sex in a manner that is appropriate to your child's age and to the situation at hand.*

Many parents have a rough-draft "sex lecture" in reserve for just that moment when their school-age child comes to them and says, "Tell me about sex." While it's a good idea to anticipate what your child may want and need to know about sex and to prepare yourself accordingly, you don't want to intimidate, embarrass, or bore your child with stiff, out-of-the-ordinary lecturelike material. And while most school-age children occasionally do come to their parents with sex-related questions, it's a rare child who ever bluntly says, "Tell me about sex."

Whether your child introduces the subject of sex or you bring it up, conduct any discussion in a natural, informal manner. Don't feel you have to go into details (e.g., about how reproduction works) unless your child seems interested. A six-year-old child may be old enough, and attentive enough, only to grasp the fact that "Daddy's penis puts a seed into Mommy's vagina." By contrast, a ten-year-old child is generally intelligent enough—and curious enough—to learn the whole basic process, from conception and fertilization to birth.

In addition to being appropriately responsive to your child's questions about sex, you also need to take the initiative in informing your child about certain sex-related matters. Your child needs to be told about such subjects as not masturbating in public, respecting other people's privacy (particularly in regard to sex play with peers), and avoiding situations that could lead to being sexually abused or sexually abusive. Don't wait for your child to say something if you feel the time is right.

Generally, the earlier you talk with your child about sex, the better. However elementary your initial discussions of it may be, they pave the way for easier, more productive discussions later on.

Children develop more self-consciousness the older they get, and so it becomes more difficult with each passing year to start talking about sex. A child over ten years old may conceal ignorance about sex in a desire to appear more sophisticated. By the time a child is sexually active, which could be as early as age eleven, she or he is bound to be acutely uncomfortable, if not downright resistant, to having any sort of discussion about sex with her or his parents.

■ *Avoid being preachy.*

You *do* need to give your child guidance in handling sexual desires and sexual pressures in a responsible manner. You *do not* need to scare your child about sex or issue threats about what will happen if your child doesn't do what you'd like her or him to do. This latter approach to such an extremely sensitive area of your child's life can only be counterproductive, inspiring possible resentment and rebellion in your child's teenage years.

■ *Relate sexual matters to everyday life.*

The best way to avoid appearing as if you're giving a lecture about sex instead of simply talking about it is to connect what you are saying with what your child has witnessed or experienced in the real world. Using specific references in this way also helps your child apply what you've said constructively to her or his own life.

For example, in talking about the love and responsibility associated with having a sexual relationship, you might allude to a recent wedding that your child attended, to the recent birth of a baby that she or he remembers, or to the lyrics in a song that your child likes. This enables her or him to think of these matters in a more respectful and understanding light. Of course, given this same discussion, you might also refer to your own relationship with your spouse or to your child's own birth, depending on how comfortable you and your listener are about discussing such personal topics.

In this type of conversation, as in any conversation relating to sex, never worry about putting ideas into your child's head. You can safely assume that more ideas—and more potentially troublesome ones—are already there than you can possibly match.

■ *Don't tease your child about her or his sexual or affectionate interests.*

A crush or a case of puppy love is a serious business for your school-age child. Through this kind of emotional attachment, a child learns to recognize and cope with all sorts of feelings related to her or his sexuality, including tenderness, yearning, devotion, despair, possessiveness, and jealousy. Dismissing or trivializing such an experience can not only rob it of its educational value but also cause significant emotional turmoil.

When your school-age child develops a romantic attraction to someone else, even a celebrity that your child has little chance of ever meeting, try to provide the freedom for your child to indulge in the attraction without comment from you. Step in only if the indulgence seems to be taking up too much of your child's time and energy or if it's creating serious problems for the love object (which is unlikely, because such attractions are usually nurtured in private).

■ *Handle incidents of sex play calmly and sensitively.*

While "show me" or "doctor" games are much more prevalent among preschoolers, children between the ages of six and ten may play them from time to time, even with members of the same sex. By far the most likely motive for such games is simple curiosity rather than erotic interests, just as it is for preschoolers.

Over the age of ten, children are typically too self-conscious to play sex games with members of the opposite sex. However, isolated incidents of sex games with members of the same sex are relatively common up to puberty and, like similar sex games at an earlier age, do not necessarily indicate that the children involved are gay.

If you catch your school-age child engaging in sex play or hear that your child has engaged in it, avoid overreacting. Instead, speak frankly and firmly with your child about the matter, advising that such activity is not appropriate and making sure she or he knows about sex and sexual responsibility. The mere fact that you've discovered what your child has done will probably embarrass her or him enough to put an end to future sex play.

Naturally, if a particular incident of sex play includes actual intercourse, abuse, or injury, you need to take stronger disciplinary action, perhaps in concert with the parents of the other child involved. Just remember at all times that your child is extremely vulnerable to becoming emotionally upset whenever her or his sexuality is at issue. With this in mind, do everything possible to help your child (1) retain her or his dignity and (2) *want* to behave more appropriately.

■ *Steer your child away from using sexual terms as swear words.*
Most children go through periods of using sexual terms as expletives or attention getters. Whenever you overhear their use, calmly let your child know that she or he is using the particular sex-related word or expression in a wrong and offensive manner. If necessary, explain exactly what the word or expression means. In any event, assure your child's promise not to misuse that particular word or expression, or any other word or expression relating to sex, in the future.

■ *Always indicate that you trust your child to handle sexual situations in a responsible manner.*
The most powerful incentive your child can have for behaving in a sexually responsible manner is your trust and positive expectations. Never permit your child to think that she or he is incapable of good behavior or that you don't have much faith in her or his judgment in sexual matters.

In situations when you do need to discipline your child for sexual misconduct, take special pains to criticize the act itself, not your child. And in any discussion you have with your child about sex, communicate your confidence in her or him to successfully manage any sex-related difficulties.

A Timetable for Sexuality: The Middle Years

Few aspects of a school-age child's emotional life vary more from child to child than sexual feelings and behaviors. Despite the enormous peer pressure on school-age children to regard and act out their sexuality in a certain manner, year after year individual kids may secretly harbor their own distinctive attitudes and pursue their own unique interests.

Nevertheless, here's a schedule describing how a child *commonly* manifests her or his sexuality at different ages during the middle years:

SIX TO SEVEN YEARS

■ efforts at strengthening personal identity through embracing gender stereotypes both in play activities and real life

■ claims to dislike peers of the opposite sex

■ heterosexual sex play to satisfy curiosity about genitals

■ interest in babies and how they are produced

■ crushes on adults (such as teachers and friends of the family)

SEVEN TO NINE YEARS

■ use of sex-related language to swear and to attract attention

■ waning of sex play

■ self-consciousness about nudity

■ dawning of prurient interest in sex

■ crushes on nonreciprocating peers

NINE TO ELEVEN YEARS

■ renewal of efforts to embrace gender stereotypes and claims to dislike the opposite sex

■ use of smutty jokes and gestures

■ drawing of naked figures and sex-related images

- increased scientific interest in sexuality and reproduction
- crushes on peers of same sex (sometimes reciprocated)
- same-sex sex play
- puppy love with peers of the opposite sex

ELEVEN TO THIRTEEN YEARS

- increased capacity for romantic attachments to peers
- increased self-consciousness about nudity
- sexual teasing, aimed both at members of the same sex and members of the opposite sex
- interest in pornography
- crushes on adults (such as celebrities)
- possible beginning of puberty
- possible beginning of sexual activity

Sexual Abuse in the Middle Years

Beginning around age six, a child is socially mature enough to associate "wrongness" with even the gentlest sexual fondling by someone else. Accompanying this sensation are all sorts of potentially traumatic emotions: feelings of fear, powerlessness, guilt, dirtiness, and worthlessness. Thus, *any* action on the part of someone else that is intentionally aimed at engaging a six- to ten-year-old child in sexual activity or is designed to sexually stimulate that child can be considered a sexually abusive act.

Sometimes abused school-age children manifest their negative emotions in a psychological way right after the abuse, for example, in nightmares or in excessive panic at being left alone. At other times, the emotions lie dormant until later in life, perhaps puberty, when the child more fully realizes what has happened. At this point, the buried emotions tend to surface behaviorally as well as psychologically. Besides having

low self-esteem, the formerly abused child may reject sex altogether, seek sex compulsively, or become a sexual abuser
her- or himself. Indeed, a high percentage of known abusers
were abused as children.

If the sexual abuser is someone the school-age child knows
and trusts, the possibility for trauma is compounded. Trapped
between her or his regard for this person and the negative
emotions already mentioned, the abused child may develop
life-crippling feelings of betrayal, mistrust, and anger. If the
abuser is a member of the family, the abused child may also
feel jealousy, shame, or hatred in relationship to other family
members.

Other situational factors influence how great the psychological aftermath of sexual abuse may be for a school-age child.
Assuming abusive episodes occurred repeatedly over an extensive period of time or frequently over a short period of time,
the emotional damage is more likely to be severe and long-
lasting. The same holds true if there were multiple perpetra-
tors of abuse, if the abuse involved coercion, terrorizing, or
pain, or if the abuser enforced secrecy.

On the positive side, effective parental response to the sexual abuse of a school-age child can do much to minimize and
even eliminate many of the damaging emotional and behavioral consequences of the abuse, no matter how severe it was.
Parents can also do a great deal to help prevent such abuse in
the first place or to put an end to it before it gets worse.

Here are some important steps to follow relating to the sexual abuse of children in their middle years:

■ *Make sure that your child is well informed about sex.*
Knowledge that links the mechanics of sexual activity to appropriate sex-related emotions, situations, and responsibilities
will help your child recognize and prevent sexual abuse when
it threatens to happen. In the event that sexual abuse should
take place anyway, this knowledge will help your child understand what has happened and discuss it with you and other
people who can assist her or him to recover from it. The earlier
this ongoing process of sexual education begins, the better. If
you're not sure how to manage the specifics of such a dialogue,
seek advice from some trustworthy, knowledgeable person who
knows your child (such as a teacher or clergyperson) or, better
still, a child psychologist or psychiatrist.

■*Advise your child when—and how—to reject physical contact.*

Assuming your child is relatively well informed about sex, considering her or his age, you can caution your child about letting other people take liberties with her or his body. You don't want to bring up abuse possibilities and strategies *every* time you discuss sex or you'll be encouraging your child to think of it as something scary in itself. But you do *occasionally* want to talk about abuse when you can work it naturally into the conversation.

First and foremost, your child should know that her or his body is private, especially the sexual areas. Then tell your child that whenever someone touches her or him in a way that feels "funny," "strange," or "not nice," she or he should immediately say no, get away from that person, and talk to you about the matter as soon as possible.

Don't worry if your child possibly misjudges innocent gestures from family members and friends. Any harm done by such misjudgments is easily remedied compared to the harm that can be done if your child reserves judgment.

■*Be alert for signs that your child has been sexually abused.*

Among these signs are the following:

■ inexplicable bruises or scratches, especially in the genital area;

■ sudden preoccupation with sex or with her or his body;

■ sudden preoccupation with sexual themes in games, language, or drawings;

■ dramatic increase in nightmares and fearful episodes (especially a fear of being left alone);

■ dramatic loss of spiritedness and self-esteem; and

■ inexplicable incidents of self-punishment.

If you observe any of the signs and suspect child abuse, express your concern to your child about her or his physical and emotional condition. Then give your child the chance to talk about anything that's bothering her or him without forcing the issue and without putting words into her or his mouth.

■ *Take seriously and pursue any reference your child makes to having been sexually abused.*

If your child makes any comment that indicates to you that she or he may have been sexually molested, give her or him your full attention and calmly but firmly encourage her or him to tell you more. Regard as truthful anything about sexual abuse that your child says to you. The odds that she or he would lie about such a disturbing matter are extremely small.

■ *Allow your child every freedom and opportunity to discuss incidents of sexual abuse as she or he chooses, without pressure.*

Don't badger your child into talking when you meet resistance and don't attach limits or cautionary terms to what your child can say. It's very difficult for children to speak about sexual abuse and you don't want to risk inadvertently causing them to refuse to speak at all.

Letting your child discuss what happened whenever—and however—she or he chooses accomplishes two important functions: It helps your child discharge her or his bad feelings about the incident, and it gives you special insights into your child's mechanisms for processing emotions.

■ *Calmly and firmly reassure your child about her or his personal worth and safety.*

Tell your child that the abuse was not her or his fault and has no effect on her or his value as a person. Also, don't forget to commend your child's bravery, honesty, and virtue in bringing the abuse to your attention.

As soon as possible, let your child know in no uncertain terms that you will do everything in your power to ensure that she or he is safe from being abused again. More than anything else at the moment, your child needs to hear you make this commitment in order to be convinced that she or he has been right to confide in you.

■ *Contact the proper authorities immediately.*

You need to honor your pledge of safety to your child by making sure you have every possible support when and if it is needed. If the suspected abuse has occurred *within* the family, contact your local Child Protection Agency. If it has occurred *outside* the family, contact your local police department or district attorney's office.

Anyone reporting to these agencies in good faith is immune

from prosecution. They will advise you about what steps you can, or should, take next.

■ *Take your child for a physical exam and a psychological evaluation.*

A visit to a medical doctor is always a good idea in cases of child abuse. Even when there are no outward signs of physical abuse, a medical examination can make certain that there is no internal physical damage or sexually transmitted disease. It can also alleviate any doubts as to the child's medical or physical condition that may emerge later on in life.

Also, since a child between the ages of six and thirteen is old enough to know that there was something wrong in what happened, it's always a good idea to get a psychological evaluation from a qualified doctor or therapist. Even if the child appears to be handling the situation pretty well, you want to do everything possible to identify any underlying psychological trauma connected with the abuse and to forestall any future development of abuse-related emotional problems.

Coping with Puberty

Puberty, the emergence of secondary sexual characteristics, can occur anytime between the ages of nine and fifteen. For females, the onset of menstruation usually takes place between twelve and fourteen years old; for males, fertility occurs between thirteen and fifteen years old.

The emotional stress directly caused by *hormonal changes* during puberty has been greatly exaggerated in popular mythology. Far more significant is the emotional stress triggered by *social issues* accompanying puberty. With all the changes they're experiencing in their bodies, children going through puberty can become very worried about peer reaction. And because their self-esteem is so wrapped up in how their peers regard them, this worry can't help but affect how they feel about themselves personally.

Puberty-related problems are more prevalent—and more severe—when puberty comes earlier than the norm. For a girl, this might be anytime between the ages of nine and twelve; for a boy, between the ages of eleven and thirteen. What makes early puberty more troublesome for the children going through it is that they are even more at odds with their peers, thus increasing the chances that they'll feel like outsiders.

A girl experiencing early puberty typically suffers much more than a boy, again for social reasons. Western culture tends to encourage boys to become men as soon as possible and, once they have, to revel in their virility. Girls, on the other hand, are taught to prize innocence, sweetness, and virginity—all characteristics of prepubescent children. Womanhood is associated not so much with power as it is with onerous hygiene matters attending menstruation, along with greater vulnerability and an unwelcome need to be especially circumspect in behavior. Illegitimate and unfair as such biases are, parents can't ignore their continuing prevalence in, and impact on, society as a whole.

Here are some guidelines for helping your child adjust to puberty, whenever it comes and regardless of how it is received by the social world outside your family:

■ *Don't tease your child about puberty.*

Remember that your child is acutely sensitive about the image she or he is projecting to other people during this period of change. She or he can easily, and unpredictably, misinterpret even the most well meaning jests about her or his newly emerging identity. And she or he can be very skillful at concealing any hurt you may have caused.

■ *Don't assume that puberty automatically means your child is more mature mentally, emotionally, or socially.*

Your child will have enough problems simply coming to terms with puberty. Don't expect her or him to take on more adult behaviors and responsibilities right away. Society at large doesn't even treat an idividual as an adult until she or he is twenty-one years old. Instead, allow your child to mature at approximately the same rate as she or he did prior to puberty.

■ *Assist your child in developing self-esteem and social poise.*

Without being pushy, make an extra effort to encourage your child to engage in *solitary* activities that she or he performs well and that give her or him gratification. Doing so will help your child maintain an ongoing sense of competency, value, and pleasure as her or his body and social image changes.

Simultaneously, and again without being pushy, help your child seek information, instruction, and experiences that will enhance *social* skills. For example, you might try interesting

her or him in reading young-adult-oriented books or periodicals, taking athletic lessons, attending summer camp, or participating in a young-adult environmental action project or
hobby club.

■ *Treat puberty as a cause for joy.*
Take pride in the fact that your child has reached puberty and
let her or him know that you feel proud. In discussing puberty
with your child, present it as a desirable and positive stage of
growth—linked with beauty, power, and a rich new range of
feelings.

QUESTIONS AND ANSWERS

GENDER STEREOTYPES

■ *In what ways are children in the middle years inclined
to exhibit gender stereotypes?*
One of the major stereotypes associated with females is that
they are inherently more sensitive and caring toward others
than males. There is no scientific evidence that such traits are
inborn; however, there is overwhelming experiential evidence
that female behavior does generally conform to the stereotype.

Girls who are age six or older are mentally capable of appreciating the fact that they may someday bear children. Along
with this appreciation comes a natural predilection toward
"mothering" and caretaking. Thus, while females may not be
genetically programmed to be more interested than males in
interpersonal relationships and more compassionate than
males while in them, school-age girls inevitably do tend to
exhibit such characteristics.

In the wake of this basic gender dissimilarity follows a
host of other more or less inevitable differences. Around the
ages of six through eight, boys tend to discharge their aggressive or anxious feelings through combative games (such
as gunplay). Girls, by contrast, tend to discharge similar feelings through role-playing games (such as "doll-baby" or
"house") or within the context of their ongoing relationships
with others (e.g., by teasing, arguing, or verbally manipulat-
ing). This doesn't mean that boys don't also play house or girls
cops and robbers occasionally. It simply points to a *tendency*
that has the appearance of inevitability.

Around the ages of nine through twelve, both boys and girls tend to discharge their aggressive or anxious feelings within the context of their ongoing relationships with others, but they do so in stereotypically different ways. Girls tend to discuss such feelings relatively openly among each other or to work them into what is otherwise a fairly cooperative dialogue. Boys, however, tend to hide such feelings, translating them instead into efforts aimed either at dominating relationships or maintaining a safe personal distance within relationships.

Aside from these rather entrenched gender stereotypes, there are others that are commonly enacted by school-age children much more voluntarily and that have much less validity. These stereotypes are mythologies about masculinity and femininity that are perpetuated by our culture; and because the latter is male dominated, they tend to present a biased image of females as submissive.

Among these culturally imposed stereotypes regarding a child's emotional life are the following:

■ Girls are naturally disposed to behave well and obey rules; boys are not.

■ Boys like sports; girls do not.

■ Girls enjoy dressing and grooming themselves; boys do not.

■ Boys prefer doing chores outside the house; girls, inside.

■ Girls are inclined to be afraid and to cry; boys are not.

■ Boys derive satisfaction from working with their hands; girls do not.

■ Girls need to express and receive a great deal of affection; boys do not.

■ Boys are emotionally tough; girls are not.

■ *How harmful is it for children to indulge in stereotypical behavior?*

Adapting to a *stereotype* is always potentially harmful in the sense that it replaces behaving according to one's *personal* identity and the *personal* identity of others. Some stereotypes may arguably be more harmful than others. For example, the stereotype that boys do not cry may cause more pain in the life of a school-age boy than the notion that boys prefer working outdoors rather than indoors. However, there is no such thing as a *good* stereotype.

By definition, a stereotype is a simplified, standardized image of a particular subject. To regard individuals, or categories of individuals (such as gender groups), in a simplified or standardized manner is always to diminish them. And to behave in accordance with a stereotype is always suspect, making it even more difficult to distinguish where one's own identity ends and a robotlike identity imposed on one by the outside world begins.

In the case of school-age children, however, some allowances for stereotypical attitudes and behaviors relating to gender need to be made. Children in the middle years are just beginning to develop self-sufficient social skills. Having relatively weak personal identities due to their continuing dependence on their parents and wanting to relate to each other as quickly, easily, and thoroughly as possible, they are irresistibly drawn toward imitating the gender stereotypes they see all around them. This grants them a certain measure of emotionally healthy security.

More to the point, demanding that a child forsake *all* stereotypical attitudes and behaviors during this formative stage in their lives can cause more emotional stress than its worth. Although it is definitely a good idea to steer children away from stereotypical attitudes and behaviors, such a policy works best when you reserve serious educational or disciplinary intervention for occasions when it's especially necessary: for example, when your child has hurt someone else's feelings or has stated a belief that is patently untrue.

Always remember that your child's attitudes and behaviors during the years between six and thirteen are largely experimental. As long as you set a good example as parents and do what you reasonably can to help your child appreciate the difference between gender stereotypes and personal realities, she or he will most likely outgrow a great deal of the predilection toward gender stereotypes.

■ *What specific things can parents do to discourage stereotypical behavior in their children?*

Aside from stepping in tactfully whenever your child has done or said something that is particularly offensive, here are some other things you can do:

■ Don't make general statements that suggest gender stereotypes, like "Be a man!" or "Girls don't carry on like that."

■ Avoid setting up stereotypes—directly or indirectly—in parenting your child. In two-parent households, fathers and mothers should share, and occasionally swap, caretaking tasks. In one-parent households, every effort should be made to involve an adult of the opposite sex in some of the caretaking tasks.

■ Use television programs, movies, news stories, and everyday incidents as contexts for discussing sexism.

■ Try interesting your child in points of view or activities that counter gender stereotypes. For example, expose your son to ballet; and if he shows interest, follow through with lessons. Or shoot baskets with your daughter; if she shows interest, find a basketball team for her to join.

■ Assuming your child is relatively indifferent, resist the tendency to buy clothes, toys, furniture, or personal items for her or him that conform to gender stereotypes (e.g., caveman T-shirts, toy trucks, rustic bunk beds, and tiger-striped notebooks for boys, as opposed to flowered T-shirts, dolls, canopied beds, and kitten-print notebooks for girls).

■ Assuming your child is otherwise happy and healthy, don't succumb to stereotypical attitudes and behaviors yourself by worrying about your child's "masculinity" or "femininity" or by pushing her or him to conform more closely to a stereotype of either. Let your child find her or his own way in this highly sensitive area of emotional life.

Allowing your child this kind of happy and healthy emotional freedom means being no more disturbed by homosexual crushes, sex play, and puppy love than you are by heterosexual crushes, sex play, and puppy love. A child's affectional experimentation during this age range should not be taken as a sign of her or his basic sexual orientation. Even more important, a child shouldn't be forced to regard homosexual feelings, let alone a homosexual orientation, as intrinsically negative.

2.

Fear

C ompared to the early years, the middle years in a child's emotional life are much less plagued by fears and phobias. The school-age child possesses more knowledge about what fear is and how it develops and is more experienced in dealing with specific fears. This knowledge and experience enable the child to confront and process typical fears during the middle years fairly effectively, at least on a subconscious level.

On the other hand, when school-age children *do* have seriously disturbing fears, they are much more likely to hide them from their parents than are younger children. The same desire to appear more mature that helps school-age children get over their fears can also make them ashamed to reveal them.

Concealment of fear is especially common in the case of boys, who can be very sensitive to the notion that it is "unmanly" to be fearful, much less to express such an emotion. Concealment is also common in the case of boys and girls who are highly success oriented. In their minds, to admit to being fearful is to acknowledge failure of some sort.

Contributing to this potential information gap between parent and school-age child is that the child is no longer at home and observable as much as she or he was during preschool years. Thus, it is easier for parents not only to miss literally seeing their child suffer from a given fear but also to lose some of their "sixth sense" insight into their child's emotional frame of reference.

Along with the estrangement from their child, parents must also cope with alienation from the world she or he inhabits. Once children begin school and therefore enter into a comparatively active inter-personal life with peers and adults outside the home, a far greater percentage of their fears tend to be social in nature. Primarily, they worry about being unacceptable, humiliated, or left out vis-à-vis the outside community.

While these school-age "social fears" may not be as emotionally devastating as the comparatively life-and-death personal fears of pre-school years, they can still be immensely distressing and potentially harmful to the child's long-term emotional health. A school-age child may be intellectually capable of recognizing when fears are out of proportion, but prevailing circumstances may not give the child the time, space, energy, or incentive to exercise this capability. Instead, she or he may live on with the fear to the point that it becomes second nature, subtly coloring everything she or he does.

Unfortunately, from a parent's perspective, many social fears never get displayed at home. Indeed, home can become a refuge from them—a place where they don't have to be indulged. And so the fears may fester far longer than is appropriate, adversely affecting the child and the family without the parents realizing what they are actually up against.

Of course, a school-age child also remains subject to fears that take place at home. In addition to such personal ones as fear of the dark or of illness, they include variations of the social fears: the fear of being unacceptable, humiliated, or left out in regard to the family in general or to a particular member of the family.

Often these home-based fears may be quite evident and fairly easy to pinpoint. For example, a six-year-old boy who is afraid of the dark may scream at night about shadows on the wall, or an eight-year-old girl who fears a loss of parental love may cling to her parents and raise a fuss whenever they leave her behind. In these cases, the cause-and-effect progression is rather obvious.

At other times, it may be apparent that the child fears *something*, even if the precise nature of that fear can't be identified. For example, a ten-year-old boy who shuns visiting his grandparents on their farm may be afraid of them, their hired hand, crossing the high bridge on the way to the farm, the horses on the farm, or any combination of the above.

However, even home-based fears may remain entirely private and undetectable to the casual observer. A school-age child can be extremely protective of her or his personal dignity. This may lead the child to do everything possible to avoid either revealing the true nature of a fear or being in situations in which she or he may unwittingly betray that fear in the presence of others.

The key to helping a school-age child manage fears in a timely and appropriate manner is to remain as informed as possible about what is going on in her or his life. Without making your child feel that you are invading her or his privacy, maintain regular communication with other adults who are witnesses to her or his day-to-day life: teachers, caretakers, and parents of your child's friends. These individuals can provide you with valuable clues about fears that your child may have, and they can serve as valuable allies in helping your child overcome those fears.

Most important, cultivate a relationship with your child that makes it easier for you to spot fears and more comfortable for your child to talk with you about them. This requires somewhat of a balancing act between treating your child as an independent person and as your dependent. You need not only to give your child a certain amount of freedom to endure fears without you but also to make sure that your child isn't burdened with more fear than she or he can properly handle.

Here are some suggestions for helping your school-age child discuss and manage her or his fears:

■ Be more of a listener than a talker.

The single most important thing you can do for your fearful child is to be a good listener. It will give you a much better understanding of what's bothering her or him and why.

Children have their own, often roundabout way of getting to the heart of the matter in conversation. Unless you give them a full opportunity to express themselves without cutting them off or putting words in their mouth, you may jump to the wrong conclusions about the nature of their fear. Worse, you may discourage them from confiding in you in the future.

To be a good listener, practice these three behaviors:

1. Concentrate on being receptive to what your child has to say instead of thinking about what you are going to say—or do—in response. Stay focused on both the actual words she or he is using and the nonverbal communication that accompanies them, such as facial expressions, body movements, posture, and eye contact.

2. Wait until your child has clearly finished saying all that she or he has to say before making any comments of your own, even if it means putting up with long, silent pauses in the conversation.

3. Periodically paraphrase what your child has said, both to make sure you've understood it correctly and to encourge your child to elaborate.

For example, suppose your child says, "I'm afraid to play ball with those guys. They're too rough." You might paraphrase this statement by saying, "So you think you might get hurt if you play ball with these guys." Your child may respond by saying, "Yes! They push and shove and run into people." Or your child may say, "Well, if I do something wrong, they yell at me." Either response moves both of you closer to the real truth about the fear.

■ *Acknowledge the pain that your child's fear is causing her or him to feel.*

Whether or not you think your child's fear is justifiable, let your child know that you understand that she or he is troubled. If appropriate, you might acknowledge that you, too, are sometimes fearful of the same situation.

■ *Assist your child in putting her or his fear into perspective.*

Begin by getting your child to express each fear-related incident in as much detail as possible (without suffering undue discomfort) so that these incidents are fully realistic in both of your minds. Then ask her or him to compare these incidents, using such questions as:

What was the worst incident to handle? Why?

What was the easiest incident to handle? Why?

The answers to these questions may give you leads regarding the main factors contributing to the fear and how to deal with it.

Another strategy to consider is to ask your child to compare this fear to other fears—real and/or hypothetical. You might also ask your child to rate this fear according to a certain scale, such as a one-to-ten scale on a mutually generated scale of awfulness. This latter activity can even inject some healthy humor into the situation—by no means to belittle your child but certainly to diminish the impact of the fear on your child.

■ *Steer your child toward facing and outgrowing her or his fear in step-by-step stages.*

After you've discussed the fear itself in sufficient depth to satisfy both of you, be sure to discuss what can be done to manage it. This discussion should be both soothing and pragmatic.

Solicit suggestions first. If your child doesn't have any suggestions to offer, then put forward your own suggestions in such a manner that she or he is free to choose among them. Before you finish your discussion, you should agree on *some* strategy and timetable, even if it's very general.

Assuming your child doesn't voluntarily propose tackling the fear head-on and right away, the best way to approach overcoming the fear is slowly but surely. Suggest an appropriate first step toward getting over the fear and get your child to agree to take that step.

For example, if your child fears heights, you might consider a picnic together near some not-so-high overlook. If your child fears failing at school, you might consider helping her or him concentrate on doing a particular assignment well, mastering a particular subject, or completing a special project that will earn special recognition. Then proceed from this initial plateau to others, being careful to let your child set the pace.

In the event that the two of you can't develop a general strategy for tackling a particular fear, try setting up an open-ended self-evaluation instrument. Your child can then use it with or without your collaboration, according to her or his preference and to your need to know how she or he is progressing.

For younger kids during the middle years (ages six to nine), this instrument may consist of a graph marking out individual days or weeks. As time goes by, your child can affix different-colored stars to particular days or weeks, according to how well the fear was managed: gold for no fear at all, silver for a little fear, red for a lot of fear, or any other system that seems appropriate.

For older kids (ages nine through twelve), a more sophisticated program can be set up: for example, a series of standard questions relating to fear management that can be answered in writing each week. Sample questions might include the following:

- How many times did I have this fear during the past week?

- How would I list them, in order of how bad they were (number 1 being the worst)?

- For each time, what was the fear like, and how did I handle it?

- For each time, how might I have handled this fear better?

- What did I learn this week about my fear and about how to handle it?

- *Be especially patient and optimistic about your child's progress in dealing with her or his fear.*

You should definitely encourage your child to confront and master her or his fears. You should perhaps even nudge your child gently and tactfully toward doing so if she or he seems to be stuck in a pattern of denial or avoidance. However, don't be too insistent if she or he refuses to follow through on your encouragement and nudging.

The more your child takes it upon her- or himself to conquer the fear, the better. Too much pressure from you can easily backfire, making her or him even more anxious and hopeless in regard to the fear.

Try at all times to pull rather than push. Express confidence in your child's ability to work through the fear; praise all efforts made and reward each victory.

As a general rule, allow your child several weeks to learn to cope with the fear, assuming it isn't causing too much disruption in the life of your child, you, or your family. Be available to provide solace or help if your child requests it, but otherwise play the more or less passive role of an observer.

When a fear persists at about the same level of severity for longer than a couple of months, more direct intervention is warranted. Perhaps there are seriously disturbing emotional issues underlying the fear. If you have reason to believe that this is the case, consider getting a professional evaluation and, possibly, professional help.

■ *Set a good example.*

School-age children expect to be taught how to do things. Often the basis for a school-age child's fear—or a major catalyst for that fear— is ignorance: What can happen to me in this situation? What's the best thing to do to get through this situation?

As a parent, you are the most influential teacher. Let your child watch you managing situations that she or he fears. Don't just give advice; literally show your child how to act out that advice. For example, if your child fears the ocean, offer ample opportunity to see you swimming in the ocean: first, near the shore in relatively calm water, and later, farther out from shore among bigger waves.

In addition to this kind of specifically targeted behavior modeling, try as hard as possible to exhibit self-confidence and bravery whenever your child is around, regardless of the situation at hand. It's also a good idea to arrange occasions when your child can observe you demonstrating bravery in the course of performing activities that you enjoy (e.g., playing basketball, painting on a ladder, or taking an active part in a social gathering).

Sometimes even setting a good example might not go all the way toward getting your child to overcome her or his fear. This is especially true in cases involving a fear of failure.

Suppose, for example, that your child remains afraid of ice-skating no matter how well you demonstrate that there is little to fear. It may be much easier for your child to overcome this fear if you entrust her or him to an expert coach, away from your watchful eyes. It isn't that your example didn't help; it's just that your child has an additional problem besides fear of ice-skating: namely, fear of embarrassment and of disappointing you.

A Timetable for Fears

Children during the middle years typically experience different types of fears at different stages in their physical, cognitive, and emotional development. Among the most prevalent age-appropriate fears are the following:

SIX TO SEVEN YEARS

■ strange, loud, or abrupt noises (e.g., animal noises, telephone and alarm ringing, wind and thunder sounds)

■ ghosts, witches, and other "supernatural" beings

■ bodily injury

■ separation from parents and being lost

■ being alone at night (and having nightmares or visitations from "evil" creatures)

■ going to school (so-called school phobia)

■ physical harm from, or rejection by, specific individuals at school

SEVEN TO EIGHT YEARS

■ the dark and dark places (such as closets, attics, and basements)

■ real-life catastrophes suggested by television, the movies, and books (e.g., kidnapping, floods, fires, nuclear attack)

■ not being liked

■ being late for school or left out of school or family events

■ physical harm from, or rejection by, specific individuals at school

EIGHT TO NINE YEARS

■ personal humiliation

■ failure in school or play

■ being caught in a lie or misdeed

■ being the victim of physical violence (either from known people or from strangers; either deliberately or randomly motivated)

■ parents fighting, separating, or being hurt

NINE TO ELEVEN YEARS

■ failure in school or sports

■ becoming sick

■ specific animals (especially animals larger than humans or those known to attack them)

■ heights and sensations of "vertigo" (e.g., dizziness)

■ sinister people (e.g., killers and molesters)

ELEVEN TO THIRTEEN YEARS

■ failure in school, sports, or social popularity

■ looking and acting "strange"

■ death or life-threatening illness or disease

■ sex (attracting others, repelling others, being attacked)

■ being fooled or "brainwashed"

■ losing possessions, being robbed

3.
Discipline

Most parents of "difficult" preschoolers secretly look forward to the school-age years as a well-deserved era of calm after the storm. They assume that their children will be more amenable to reason in matters of discipline and that the schooling experience itself will teach them better self-control and more appropriate behaviors in addition to academic knowledge.

In reality, parents of preschoolers are well justified in harboring such hopes. But in their eagerness to envision the new *positive* possibilities that can accompany this stage of a child's life, they tend to overlook the new *negative* ones.

The school-age years are, indeed, generally characterized by a more sophisticated dialogue between parent and child relating to acceptable versus nonacceptable behavior. And the schooling experience typically helps socialize children and make them more responsible for their own conduct and success in life. However, the same mental and emotional growth that enables school-age children to be more *mature* in their conversations and behaviors also emboldens them to be more *devious* in their conversations and behaviors.

In disciplining your child between the ages of six and thirteen, keep in mind that she or he is going through a period of frequent and often intense criticism affecting every aspect of life. This criticism ranges from formal grades on intellectual performance to informal peer evaluations of her or his desirability as a playmate or companion to family judgments about what kind of individual she or he is turning out to be: mentally, physically, morally, and emotionally.

Furthermore, this criticism is no longer tempered by the kinds of indulgent smiles and gushes that a preschooler so easily inspires, even when misbehaving. Instead, the school-age child is expected to act like an adult-in-training—someone who is now a serious individual in her or his own right and who is accountable for every failing.

In order to adjust to this climate of criticism and then to live within it, the school-age child develops many different coping mechanisms. Among the most prevalent is what is known in psychological terms as "acting out" behavior: that is, "undisciplined" behavior prompted by an overpowering need to relieve anxiety, express displeasure, rebel against control, or simply cry out for help.

Thus, while a specific act of bad, incompetent, or inappropriate behavior may have a simple explanation, it may also have a very complicated one. And while conversation with your child may help you understand misbehavior, it may also set up a smoke screen. In a conscious or subconscious effort at self-defense, your child can now use her or his emerging verbal and social skills to mislead you whenever such a strategy seems necessary.

For example, a school-age boy who persists in damaging the furniture when he plays in the house, despite repeated parental discipline, may have legitimate difficulty in managing his basic exuberance. On the other hand, he may be wrecking the furniture as an indirect means of attacking his parents' "unacceptable" bedtime rules. In the latter case, whether or not he realizes his true motivation, he may blame the damage on a sibling or on an innocent accident.

Similarly, a school-age girl who continually fails to learn better table manners may sincerely have a problem concentrating on manners amid other mealtime distractions. Alternatively, she may be refusing to use good table manners just to have the final say in *some* aspect of her life, even if it isn't a very important one. Whatever the case, she may try to thwart her parents' disciplinary efforts by feigning incompetence, lack of hunger, or illness.

Given these two key factors in the lives of school-age children—(1) the amount of criticism typically directed toward them and (2) the potential complexity and elusiveness of their real motives for misbehavior—parents of school-age children need to be especially discriminating in deciding *when* and *how* to manage individual disciplinary issues. In more colloquial terms, they need to make sure they look before they leap.

This overall approach to discipline involves a great amount of patience and observation. You need to reserve criticism and disciplinary action for especially serious situations, letting minor annoyances and infractions pass without comment. Any school-age child can easily suffer emotional turmoil from too many "dos" and "don'ts," no matter how gently these "dos" and "don'ts" are offered.

Moreover, you need to avoid jumping to conclusions about what has occurred and why. Respect the fact that life has become more complicated for your school-age child and allow her or him the benefit of the doubt whenever possible, as well as every opportunity to express and explain her or his feelings. Remember that ultimate responsibility—and reward—as a parent is not to discipline your child but to help your child discipline her- or himself.

Here are some additional guidelines for managing disciplinary matters involving your school-age child:

■ *Be as specific as possible about what you want—or don't want—your child to do.*

School-age children tend to hold parents to their exact words, so your directives and rules should be very clear. It isn't enough to tell a seven-year-old, "I want you to be on your best behavior when we visit Aunt Marian." Instead, the seven-year-old needs a few specific examples of what constitutes "good" as opposed to "bad" behavior. Although children are likely to tune out long-winded descriptions and explanations, they do need specific images to use in controlling their behavior.

Besides making sure that children know *what* you expect of them, you should also make sure they know *how* to meet those expectations. Whenever possible, teach them various ways in which they can control their "unacceptable" behavior, or change it, and still derive personal satisfaction.

Finally, give the reasons behind your requests and check to make sure your child understands and accepts those reasons. The more a school-age child buys into *why* a certain command or rule is being issued, the more likely she or he is to cooperate with that command or rule.

It isn't always easy to communciate reasons to be a "newly" rational child without opening up a prolonged debate. Again, patience is a necessity. The long-term benefit, however, far outweighs the short-term effort.

For convenience' sake every parent of a school-age child occasionally resorts to demanding obedience strictly "because I say so." Just try to keep these occasions to a bare minimum. If you don't, your "say-so" starts losing its effectiveness.

■ *Be honest about the possible difficulty or unpleasantness involved in what you want your child to do.*

Don't seduce your child into following a certain rule or performing a certain task by sugarcoating the consequences. Once your child finds out the truth, she or he will cease to trust you. Instead, anticipate any problems your child is likely to have with the rule or task and acknowledge those problems up front. Obviously you don't want to belabor these problems. But you also don't want to leave your child unprepared and possibly unwilling to overcome them as well as suspicious ever after of your judgment in such matters.

For example, suppose you want your child to be home from playing each day by five in the afternoon so that she or he is off the streets during rush hour and has plenty of time to get ready for dinner. After communicating this rule to your child and your reasons for making it, let her or him know that you're aware of how hard it can be to stop playing when you're having fun—but that you believe you can count on her or him to do these things even if they aren't easy.

■ Criticize your child's behavior, not your child.

When your child does something wrong, don't imply that she or he is "wrong." Instead, stay focused on the particular incident at hand and why the behavior is unacceptable.

For example, if your child throws something at you in anger, resist the temptation to yell something like "You're being a real monster today." Instead, say in a more controlled voice, "That's a very wrong thing to do," and lead her or him to understand *why*.

Children in the middle years are very sensitive about their self-worth and can be devastated by even the mildest criticism directed—intentionally or unintentionally—toward who they are. Whatever they may have done, it somehow seemed right to them at the time. Their misperception needs to be corrected; they don't need to be "corrected" as individuals.

■ Don't permit discussions involving misbehavior to escalate into arguments.

Every time you're obligated to confront your child about something "wrong" that's been done, give her or him a chance to tell you about it before you drop the matter entirely or administer punishment. Listen carefully to what your child says, without interrupting, and make sure that you understand her or his version of what happened. This can give you valuable insights into the nature of your child's ongoing emotional life as well as into the particular episode at hand.

In these discussions, also be alert to your child's *nonverbal* communication. For example, if your child avoids eye contact or fidgets excessively, it could be a sign that she or he is fearful, lying, or hiding something. Assuming that you suspect such is the case, question your child tactfully, opening up every opportunity for some information to be volunteered.

Keep discussions relatively short and simple. School-age children can be very clever at extending a dialogue, either to press their point or to forestall punishment, but a child is not yet your intellectual equal. You can't expect to reason out everything, nor can you always come to full agreement about all the issues involved in the incident.

Once you feel that you have given your child a fair chance to talk and that you have adequate knowledge about what has happened and why, bring the conversation to a close. Then make a more or less "formal" and "final" announcement of how you interpret what has happened and, if appropriate, the consequences of what she or he has or hasn't done.

■ *Make any punishment fit the misdemeanor.*

In many cases, your criticism and apparent disappointment may be sufficient punishment. Certainly this should be your goal. However, in those cases in which stronger discipline seems warranted, make every effort to relate the punishment to the particular wrongdoing.

For example, if your child creates a mess, assign her or him the job of cleaning it up. If that's not possible, suggest some other chore. If a child strikes another child, insist that she or he apologize to that child and then remain alone and quiet in her or his room for an appropriate amount of time. If a child fails to do homework or chores because she or he was watching television, don't allow any viewing for an appropriate period of time.

This strategy not only appeals to a school-age child's need for logic and justice in life but also teaches responsibility for the consequences of specific actions. If you rely on a fixed, limited repertoire of punishments—for example, consistently either denying television privileges or "grounding" your child, no matter what the offense—your child will gradually learn to tolerate such punishments (whether or not she or he lets you know it), and they will lose their deterrent power. Even worse, you will be teaching your child to see the misbehavior-punishment cycle as a ritual game that is played between the two of you.

Whenever you are disciplining a child, try to remain in firm control of your temper, your words, and your actions. Your authoritative demeanor will not only help you manage disciplinary matters as efficiently as possible without negative emotional repercussions but also set a powerful example of self-control for your child.

■ *Try never to spank or strike your child.*

Resorting to physical violence gives children a very negative example of what to do when one is losing control of her or his emotions. It also automatically provokes fear and resentment. Children have little choice but to suppress most, if not all, of this fear and resentment— a development that threatens their long-term, overall emotional well-being and damages their relationship with you.

Despite being aware of the repercussions, even the most well-meaning parents can, on occasion, get carried away and strike or spank their child, especially if they themselves received this type of discipline when they were children. In the event that you do strike or spank your child, immediately offer her or him a calm but sincere apology and proceed with another, more constructive form of punishment.

Then forgive yourself and renew your personal commitment not to let a similar loss of self-control happen again.

■ *Try to give your child more positive than negative feedback.*
The best way to motivate your child to behave well and strengthen the effectiveness of any discipline you're compelled to administer from time to time is to make sure that you *praise* more often than you *criticize* your child. Be on the lookout for commendable behavior and comment on it. At the same time, ignore behavior that isn't commendable as much as you can.

You may also try to assist your child in those activities during which she or he is most inclined to exhibit appropriate behavior or perform exceptionally well. Your child's self-esteem will be bolstered, and you will have more opportunities to bestow praise upon her or him. This technique is particularly advisable if your child is experiencing major discpline or self-confidence problems in some other aspect of her or his life.

■ *As much as possible and appropriate, coordinate your own disciplinary policies with others that your child may experience.*
Talk with all of your child's teachers about their specific disciplinary policies in the classroom as well as the general ones of the school. Also, let each of your child's teachers know about your disciplinary policies at home. Work out a "compromise" policy that helps ensure that your child's disciplinary problems are handled in a consistent manner, whether they crop up at home or in school.

It's also a good idea to inform other caretakers of your child—babysitters, relatives, or friends—about your preferred ways of administering discipline. This helps prevent your child from being treated too leniently or too abusively when you aren't there to supervise.

In addition, regularly interview your child's teachers and caretakers at some length about how your child behaves in their presence. Often disciplinary problems only arise, or disappear, in a particular interpersonal or environmental context.

If you find out that your child misbehaves when she or he is away from you, try to arrange a meeting that includes you, your child, and the teacher or caretaker who encounters this misbehavior. At this meeting, present to the child what you've been told in a loving and nonthreatening manner, ask for her or his reaction, and then discuss the problem and how to manage it, giving priority in the discussion to your child's comments and suggestions.

If such a meeting can't be arranged, then tactfully bring up the issue with your child by yourself. In the event that she or he persists in denying the accusation, take a hypothetical approach (i.e., "Supposing someone did act this way . . .") and briefly discuss the problem and the possible solutions.

Assuming you discover that your child misbehaves only in your presence, it's more diplomatic to talk about the issue with your child by yourself rather than including the teacher or caretaker who made the problem known to you. Again, be very supportive and nonthreatening and solicit your child's comment on how the situation might be improved.

■ *Set a good example.*

To a school-age child, an adult's word is only as good as her or his deed; and a school-age child is keenly observant regarding adult deeds. Anytime you and your child are together, make a special effort to practice what you preach and to be obedient to rules (including those imposed by outside authorities, such as speed limits, crossing signals, and litter laws).

QUESTIONNAIRE:

Problem Behavior in the Middle Years

Here is a two-part questionnaire you can use for two purposes:

1. to begin making distinctions between more serious and less serious discipline problems in your school-age child's life; and

2. to begin making possible connections between your school-age child's discipline problems and emotional issues contributing to, or resulting from, those problems.

First, complete "Part A: Discipline Problems," rating the degree of each problem on a scale of 1 to 5, with 5 being the most severe rating. (*Note*: Some of the listed problems overlap in certain situations.) Next, complete "Part B: Emotional Issues," rating each issue in the same manner. Then make a list of all the problems in Part A that you've rated 4 or 5 and a separate list of all of the issues in Part B that you've rated 4 or 5. Finally, draw any cause-and-effect relationships that seem relevant to you between items on your Part A, 4 or 5 rating list and items on your Part B, 4 or 5 rating list.

If you have rated ten or more items 4 or 5 in either of the original lists, then your child may be suffering from serious emotional problems. If you think this may be the case, consider seeking professional help.

PART A: DISCIPLINE PROBLEMS

1. Doesn't obey rules	1	2	3	4	5
2. Doesn't play cooperatively with siblings	1	2	3	4	5
3. Doesn't play cooperatively with peers	1	2	3	4	5
4. Creates disturbances when other adults are present	1	2	3	4	5
5. Bullies siblings or peers	1	2	3	4	5
6. Talks back to parents	1	2	3	4	5
7. Talks back to adults other than parents	1	2	3	4	5
8. Destroys property	1	2	3	4	5
9. Lies or refuses to tell the truth	1	2	3	4	5
10. Steals	1	2	3	4	5
11. Doesn't clean up own messes	1	2	3	4	5
12. Picks quarrels	1	2	3	4	5
13. Uses offensive language	1	2	3	4	5
14. Strikes out physically at others	1	2	3	4	5
15. Expresses displeasure or resentment when asked to do something	1	2	3	4	5
16. Refuses to do something when asked	1	2	3	4	5
17. Fails to do something after agreeing to do it	1	2	3	4	5
18. Blames other people for own actions	1	2	3	4	5
19. Acts disturbingly immature	1	2	3	4	5
20. Gets into fights	1	2	3	4	5

PART B: EMOTIONAL ISSUES

1. Feelings get hurt	1	2	3	4	5
2. Acts in a shy manner	1	2	3	4	5
3. Acts in an aggressive manner	1	2	3	4	5
4. Worries	1	2	3	4	5
5. Exhibits fear	1	2	3	4	5
6. Gets distracted	1	2	3	4	5
7. Seems restless	1	2	3	4	5
8. Overreacts	1	2	3	4	5
9. Goes through major mood changes	1	2	3	4	5

10.	Gets frustrated performing tasks	1	2	3	4	5
11.	Acts possessively toward parent	1	2	3	4	5
12.	Avoids parent	1	2	3	4	5
13.	Avoids sibling	1	2	3	4	5
14.	Avoids peers in general	1	2	3	4	5
15.	Avoids particular peer	1	2	3	4	5
16.	Exhibits disappointment	1	2	3	4	5
17.	Exhibits boredom	1	2	3	4	5
18.	Is unable to sustain relationships	1	2	3	4	5
19.	Exhibits hostility	1	2	3	4	5
20.	Exhibits unhappiness	1	2	3	4	5

CASE:

The Mother Tester

Danny was a bright, sensitive, loving child until he reached age eight. Almost overnight, it seemed to his mother, Susan, as if he'd been secretly appointed her special persecutor.

Whenever Susan needed to correct Danny's behavior, he screamed, "I hate you. You're the meanest mother on Earth." If she was forced to deny him something, he shrieked, "You don't love me. You don't let me have anything I really want." And yet he constantly followed her around and complained bitterly on those few occasions during the week when she tried to have some moments to herself.

Susan knew from her reading and her conversations with friends that eight-year-olds are inclined to fight with their mothers and thereby act out their own frustrations regarding dependence and control. But Danny's nonstop rebelliousness was taking too much of a toll on her time and energy, not to mention on their relationship. Was something else bothering Danny, Susan wondered, or was this simply a very intense version of the "crazy eights"?

After discussing Danny with his teacher, his baby-sitter, and other adults in the family and observing Danny's day-to-day life more closely for a couple of weeks, Susan was convinced that her son's only significant problem lay in his relationship with her. Therefore, she resolved to improve that relationship as much as possible. Together with her husband, Joe, she devised a two-part plan.

The first part of Susan's plan was to arrange Danny's schedule so that the two of them spent much more time apart from each other, at least for a few weeks. Fortunately, Danny and Joe got along with each other beautifully, and Joe was willing and able to double the time that he took charge of Danny. Even better, this time included many more hours away from home for Danny so that both Danny and his mother could have a complete and refreshing break from each other.

The other part of Susan's plan was to improve the quality of the time that she and Danny did spend together. As often as she could during these times, she gave Danny her undivided attention. She made sure to express her affection for Danny frequently and to engage him in activities that they could both enjoy, such as playing computer and card games, watching television, flying kites in the park, and raking leaves.

Soon after Susan inaugurated her two-part plan, Danny's behavior started changing for the better. He continued to attack Susan verbally from time to time. But when he did, she took it much more in stride, which, in turn, sent a message to Danny that his attack strategy wasn't really accomplishing anything.

By his ninth birthday, Danny had recovered from being an eight-year-old "rebel with a cause." Susan's plan had not eliminated that necessary stage in Danny's emotional growth, nor had it made her job as a mother any less demanding. However, her plan had made that growth period for Danny much less painful and her job as a mother much more rewarding.

At PCGC:
Treatment in a Family
Context

School-age children who have severe disciplinary or behavioral problems can't be separated from their parents for extensive treatment without suffering some degree of trauma. Furthermore, these disciplinary and emotional problems are most effectively analyzed by examining that child in the context of her or his family life rather than in the context of an isolating, institutional testing.

One solution to these difficulties is to offer a "home living" environment within the hospital or clinic: a place where the family can remain together, and function as a family, while the child's problems are being evaluated. This situation allows clinicians and treatment teams to witness the family culture in operation—either through "visits" or through one-way-mirror observations—and to apply systematically a variety of interventions in a controlled environment.

In addition to severe disciplinary and behavioral problems, issues involving school-age children that are appropriate for this kind of comprehensive, on-site care include:

■ emotional complications relating to a chronic physical illness;

■ psychosomatic disorders, such as asthma, gastrointestinal illness, or diabetes;

■ problems related to eating (including obesity and such eating disorders as anorexia or bulimia);

■ school phobia;

■ severe depression and/or suicidal behavior;

■ persistent attempts to run away;

■ a situation in which there are multiple patients within a single family.

PCGC has a Family Apartment Unit Program that offers this kind of clinical approach for school-age children and their families needing intensive psychiatric evaluation and treatment in a therapeutic setting. The family as a whole literally moves into a two-room apartment (bedroom and living room/dining and kitchen area) within the PCGC complex for professional observation and intervention on a twenty-four-hour basis.

Prior to admission of the family, there are several assessment conferences with the family and the referring therapist to clarify how the program runs and how it might be useful and to arrange a schedule for the program that suits all individuals involved. On arrival at the apartment for participation in the program, the family inevitably has to mobilize its resources to cope with the novel circumstances. This mobilization effort in itself helps to move the family toward positive change.

Once the family is fairly well established in the apartment, PCGC clinicians and treatment teams orchestrate therapeutic interventions to correspond with their observations. A "typical" family therapy session is only one of many possible interventions aimed at reorganizing the way the family functions so that it as a whole and the child in particular can better manage the latter's problem. Other possibilities include testing (medical as well as psychological), education, conflict resolution, skill training, role-playing, and behavioral modification.

The primary considerations for discharge from PCGC's Family Apartment Unit Program are whether there has been a decrease in the child's symptoms and whether the family has begun to show itself capable of modifying those patterns of interaction that have contributed to the child's problem. The overall goal in every case is for the family to learn how to take effective control of its own difficulties and how to make effective use of the outside support systems.

Check with local mental health organizations to find out if there are similar programs in your area. If not, discuss with your psychiatrist, psychologist, or mental-health professional ways to incorporate similar features into your child's therapy.

4.

Chores

Giving school-age kids chores to do at home helps them teach themselves the ways, means, and virtues of behaving responsibly. The long-term result is a lowering of stress and a heightening of self-esteem. As a bonus, performing chores instills in kids a greater appreciation for their parents' efforts at setting up and maintaining a harmonious home environment.

Some six- to twelve-year-olds take naturally to chores. They may see performing chores as a kind of adult "game," as an emotionally satisfying way of imposing order on chaos, as a source of "instant pride" and gratification, or as an extension of their love for their home and their parents. A child who falls into this category should be directed toward some of the more complicated and rewarding household activities that go beyond mere chore performance, such as cooking, gardening, car maintenance, home repair, or home decorating.

A child who expresses a sincere enthusiasm and talent for one of these activities can become an apprentice as well as a chore doer. Be careful not to force matters. Instead, keep a keen eye on your child's interests, follow her or his lead, and put everything on a voluntary basis. In the meantime, your child should still have a certain number of required chores.

Regrettably, most children between the ages of six and thirteen do not fit the above description. For numerous reasons, including simple lack of interest, they do not tend to take to chores naturally. However, if they receive firm policies, firm direction, and firm monitoring from their parents, they can learn to perform chores not only skillfully and dependably but also enjoyably.

Most children in their middle years have no choice but to participate in personal and home maintenance if the household is to function smoothly. This is especially true in the case of households with one parent or two working parents. Unless the participation is organized into clear, well-conceived, and mutually agreed-upon task assignments, it will forever give rise to disappointments, resentment, misunderstandings, quarrels, and animosities.

Assigning chores and making sure that they are performed can be an emotional battleground in itself. Parents can easily find themselves turning into dictators, at which point children inevitably cast themselves as defiant—and self-righteous—rebels.

Here are guidelines for managing chore assignments so that there is a minimum of stress and strain:

■ *Create with your child a schedule of chores that she or he needs to perform on a regular basis.*
Work together with your child to make this schedule so that both of you have input. Be as specific as you reasonably can, including days and time frames for performing individual tasks. When the schedule is finished, copy it over so that it's very neat and official looking and post it in a highly visible place in the home. You might even want to include spaces on the list for marking off each time a task has been completed.

The actual number of chores—and the duration of each one—should be tailored to fit the age of the child and the amount of free time the child has: not so many that completing all the chores satisfactorily becomes a hardship and not so few that no real sacrifice is involved. Start low and adjust the list every few months—adding, subtracting, or changing—if and when the situation seems to warrant it.

Ideally, there should be one or more tasks that the child needs to do, and that a parent can monitor, on a daily basis. "Two or three days" seems like a much longer period of time to a six- to twelve-year-old child than it does to an adult, and you don't want too much time to pass during which your child feels as if she or he has no household responsibilities. Examples of daily tasks a school-age child might perform include picking up toys and other objects from the family-room floor, setting the table, making sure that certain wastebaskets are emptied, or feeding the family pet.

■ *Assign chores that make your child feel that she or he is making an important contribution to family life.*
In addition to personally meaningful responsibilities like "clean your room," the list should include some family-oriented tasks like "wash the dishes," "clean the inside of the car," or "bind papers for recycling." Some of these tasks should be ones that the child performs completely independent of anyone else.

Be sure to solicit suggestions for family-oriented tasks from your child. You may be surprised at the number that she or he has observed or feels capable of undertaking.

Always try to let your child do any job that she or he volunteers to do, even if it means revising your normal method of doing it. Your child's spirit of initiative should be encouraged whenever possible.

If your child wants to take on a chore that you think is beyond her or his capabilities, try breaking it down into parts and giving your child one of them to do. Add parts as competence is acquired. Again, you may be surprised at your child's capabilities, given the right opportunity.

■ *Assign chores that suit your child's interests, temperament, and skills.*

Any task that your child enjoys doing will be better performed and therefore more rewarding to both you and her or him. Keep your eyes open for tasks, or parts of tasks, that might fit this category. Your child may not come up with many suggestions of her or his own, partly because she or he is not as familiar as you are with the full range of chores that need to be done.

■ *Assign some chores that you and your child can perform together.*

Working together is a wonderful way of getting to know each other better, of learning to interact more cooperatively, and of building stronger emotional bonds. Most of the chores you assign should be those that can be done without your help, but one or two could be done together. Start with easy chores—ones that allow you plenty of freedom to chat and even to play around—and then progress to those that are more complicated—ones that your child may not even be capable of tackling without your being there.

Exercise special patience with your child in these situations. Remember that your goal is not only to finish the task successfully but also to develop a good, long-term partnership. If performing a certain chore together doesn't work out after you've given it a sufficient trial, tactfully bring the experiment to an end, wait a while (a few weeks or more), and try performing another chore together: one that you feel has a better chance.

■ *Make sure that your child understands how best to perform each chore.*

Before officially assigning a task to your child, make sure she or he knows how to do it, when to do it, why it needs to be done, and what you expect as a result. Children don't respond well to lengthy directions, so be as clear and concise as you can without leaving any room for misunderstanding.

■ *As much as possible, don't do chores yourself that your child fails to do.*

Let your child see the consequences of her or his negligence. For example, if she or he forgets to set the table, keep the meal waiting until the task is accomplished. If your child doesn't empty the waste-baskets, let them overflow as long as you can until your child empties them. If your child doesn't pick up her or his toys, leave them on the floor (sliding them out of traffic paths) until she or he collects them.

■ *Establish, and stick to, appropriate procedures and penalties for not doing chores.*

At the time you first establish what chores your child is to perform, you should also tell her or him the penalty policy for nonperformance of chores. This policy should be general and flexible enough so that individual penalties can fit specific situations.

For example, you might agree on a policy of "losing time for play, television, or other personal activities." Then, assuming there comes a time when your child plays outdoors instead of doing a chore, you might ground your child for a day or require her or him to spend a certain amount of time alone in her or his room.

Make certain that your child pays an appropriate penalty, if warranted, *every time* she or he fails to perform a task, in accordance with your original understanding. And try to enforce the penalty as soon as possible after the nonperformance, preferably within a day or two.

As a general rule, it's not advisable to punish children by cutting or withholding their allowance. In the first place, it inclines them to associate doing chores with earning money instead of doing them purely for their own sake and/or for the good of the family. In the second place, being without their regular amount of money may put them at a serious and unfair disadvantage, causing them, for example, to miss a worthwhile outing with friends or to make up the shortfall by stealing, lying, or cheating.

However, if your child's misbehavior involves money (e.g., breaking a window that must be repaired), then it may well be appropriate to ask your child to pay for part, or all, of the damage. This can be done in a lump sum or in installments.

At the same time that you set up a penalty policy, you also need to establish procedures for those occasions when your child has a time conflict affecting chore performance. In cases when your child knows in advance that she or he may not—or will not—be able to do her or his chores, she or he could be required to renegotiate the chore time with you, volunteer to do some other chore at a more convenient time, or find a replacement to do the chore.

In emergency situations, when there's a good reason why the chores can't be done and advance notice can't be given, your child should be required to do everything within reason to let you know about the situation as soon as possible.

To Bribe or Not to Bribe?

A major dilemma for every parent of a school-age child is whether or not to barter money, possessions, or privileges in exchange for the child's good behavior or successful task performance. If the question doesn't first occur to the parent, it will eventually be raised by the child. And if such a bartering system prevails in the outside, adult world, why shouldn't it prevail inside the home, between parent and child?

On the one hand, this type of reward system in the home eliminates the need to wrangle over such issues as "Why should I?" School-age children are generally quite eager to strike bargains that offer them tangible benefits. If they should ultimately fail to meet their end of the bargain, the punishment is built in: They don't get the reward. Thus, a lot of time and emotionally draining energy is saved for both parent and child.

On the other hand, this type of reward system sets up a highly questionable value system. Children learn to sell their good behavior and chore-doing skills instead of offering them freely out of a sense of love, self-satisfaction, and personal responsibility. Given this "sell" mentality, the price for good behavior and chore-doing skills is bound to go up as time goes on. The result is a situation in which children can arbitrarily pick or choose when and how to be good or to do chores on their own terms—a situation filled with emotionally upsetting booby traps for parent and child alike.

Unfortunately, there is no black-and-white answer to the bribery question. What works between adults in the outside world is not *always* applicable to the parent-and-child situation inside the home, where the child is most definitely dependent on the parent both financially and in terms of the child's moral education.

However, *sometimes* what works in the outside world *is* applicable and even appropriate. Occasionally you do need to bargain with your child to achieve more than what is normally expected and your child does need to learn the positive aspects of how bargaining works in the real world.

Here are some tips for determining whether or not to bribe as well as how and what to bribe when doing so seems appropriate:

■*Above all, save bribery for very special situations.*

Don't apply it to regular chores but to one-time tasks that are unusually time consuming or undesirable. Also, allow a generous amount of time to lapse between bribe situations: at least two weeks for a six- to eight-year-old and at least a month for a nine- to twelve-year-old.

Try never to offer a bribe merely for good behavior. This strategy undermines your ability to influence your child's behavior under any circumstances *without* offering some tangible incentive.

In cases in which exceptionally good behavior is desired, you might try incorporating some task into the period during which the good behavior is to be exercised. For example, if you want to help make sure that your seven-year-old behaves well at a large family gathering, you might offer to pay your child to watch over one of the younger children there—an assignment that would include the direction not to engage in roughhousing, monopolizing adult attention, or wandering out of sight. Nevertheless, it would be much better in the long run if you could forgo bribery and give your child a chance to live up to your expectations.

■*Retain control of what the bribe is to be.*

Don't ask your child what she or he would like in exchange for doing something. You might get an answer that you don't want! Offer the child a specific bribe of your own choice at the same time that you present the assignment.

Depending on the situation, your child's emotional maturity, and the relationship you have with her or him, you might allow a small margin for bargaining *after* you've presented your offer. But know your limit ahead of time and stick to it, even if the assignment ultimately goes unaccepted. It's better to lose out one or two times than to succumb to a policy that makes you fail on a regular basis.

■*Make the reward modest and specific.*

Your child should be encouraged to work for the reward in itself and not *according to its value*. For this reason, it's not necessary or even advisable that the reward be exactly commensurate with the task from an adult-world point of view. It should simply be something that you know your child would like regardless of whether it is attached to task performance.

Be conservative in what you offer. Don't verbally set up

equations between the reward and the task (e.g., "I think this task is worth a trip to the zoo"). Instead, refer to the bribe as a treat that you are offering as a special, appreciative gesture for doing something above and beyond normal requirements. And try not to create a pattern of bribery that indirectly sets up a value scale for different types of tasks.

Also, your bribe should be something that is well defined and therefore easily visualized. This makes for a much more powerful incentive. Avoid relatively vague bribes like "I'll buy you something at the store" (what? when?) or "I'll look the job over after you're done and decide." You might be paving the way for disappointment and discouragement.

The best bribes are nonmonetary ones. They not only make for more appealing mental pictures but also don't lend themselves as easily to creating a cut-and-dried value system. Try offering specific privileges, outings, or goods. If you do offer money, offer a fixed amount, not increments per parts of the job or a sliding scale.

It's best to avoid bartering with official rules and procedures involving chores, allowance, bedtimes, television hours, and so on. A bribe should involve something entirely outside—and in addition to—the normal, assured, and reassuring scheme of things.

■ *If possible, make the reward appropriate to the request.*
While you don't want to set up a *value equation* between a task and a bribe, it helps if you can draw a *logical connection* between a task and a bribe. For example, if you want the garage cleaned out, you might promise an excursion by car. If you want the room where you watch television cleaned up, you might offer to rent a video for that night. If you want the kitchen floor mopped and waxed, you might propose making a special snack or meal. This way, the child can truly enjoy the fruits of her or his labor.

■ *Provide the reward as soon as possible after it is earned.*
To children in the middle years, more than a week away is a very long time. Live up to your end of the bargain promptly, being careful to wait until the entire task is completed. Also, don't offer the reward in advance. It may ultimately not be earned!

■ *Occasionally give surprise rewards for exceptional task performance.*
After children have been especially diligent in performing

their assigned chores over an extended period of time, it's appropriate to surprise them with some sort of tangible acknowledgment that you've noticed, and are pleased by, what they've done. A surprise reward is even more appropriate when children take it upon themselves to perform a nonrequired task or when they perform an exceptionally onerous task at your request without getting a bribe.

In these situations, the best reward is arranging to do something special together that you both enjoy, such as fishing, going out to eat, visiting an amusement park, or taking in a movie. Ideally, this treat will be just for you and your child, independent of other children in the family (unless they also have the same record of exceptional performance, and everyone can enjoy the event and each other's company during the event).

5.

Running Away

The image of a school-age child defiantly insisting that she or he will run away from home and be self-sufficient is a popular piece of Americana, inspiring amusement for parents and romantic adventure for children. The reality, however, is frightening both from the child's and the parent's point of view.

Even if a would-be runaway only pretends to make good on this threat by hiding somewhere or by fleeing to a friend's or relative's home, the emotional effect on the family of such a dramatic gesture can be very painful. The would-be runaway must forcibly confront just how isolated, dependent, and powerless she or he is, while the parent, in addition to being worried about her or his child, can't help but feel personally rejected, humiliated, and frustrated.

Once a child who has threatened to leave home actually takes to the streets, with or without any serious intentions, her or his life itself is at risk. The child's anger, hurt, and confusion make her or him exceptionally accident-prone. They also make her or him exceptionally vulnerable to suggestion and coercion; and tragically, the streets are becoming more and more populated by molesters, criminals, and opportunists who are dangerously clever at suggesting and coercing.

To prevent runaway threats from occurring or to manage them when they do occur, follow these recommendations:

■ *Keep arguments from escalating into verbal fights.*
Most threats to run away emerge in the context of heated arguments between parent and child, when the child feels she or he has no other ammunition to use. Therefore, guard against arguing to the point where you and your child are deliberately intimidating each other. If you feel things getting out of hand, stop speaking, pause, and suggest that you both take time to cool down—at least a few minutes—before resuming the conversation.

■ *Never directly or indirectly present leaving home as an option.*
Resist any temptation to dare your child to leave home or to tease your child about being incapable of surviving away from the family.

Always make it clear that you want your child to live at home because you love her or him, not just because you are responsible for her or his welfare.

Also, be careful not to draw a strong, dramatic line between home and the outside world in your child's imagination. In converations or outright arguments with your child, try never to use provocative phrases like "As long as you're living under my roof, you'll do what I say" or "Once you get out on your own, you're free to do whatever you want; but until then, you have to abide by the rules." These kinds of remarks are, in effect, offering your child a very risky choice.

■ *Always take seriously any threat your child makes to run away.*
In the vast majority of situations, a child who threatens to run away doesn't really want to leave home. Instead, she or he feels rejected or out of place at home. The threat to run away is simply a cry for recognition, love, and acceptance. If you dismiss this threat in your language or behavior, your child may feel not only doubly ignored but also doubly pressured to follow through on the threat or else lose face entirely.

For these reasons, never ridicule, deny, or treat casually any threat that your child makes about running away. Let your child know immediately, in a calm but firm voice, that you don't want her or him to run away, that it would make you very unhappy, and that you will do everything you can not to let it happen—or, if it does happen, anyway, to bring her or him back.

■ *Offer your child options to running away.*
If, during the course of day-to-day family life, you sense that your child is contemplating running away or feels in any way "crowded" or burdensome at home, take appropriate action to make her or his life within the family more satisfying. Assuming your child seems to desire more privacy, you might arrange matters so that she or he can be alone and undisturbed for a certain period of time each day or can have a room of her or his own. Assuming your child seems to desire more attention, you might give her or him a leadership role in a particular family activity.

In situations when your child literally threatens to run away, ask her or him if there isn't some other possible solution. If your child isn't forthcoming with alternatives, you might suggest getting away from each other for a while. Perhaps your child could visit a relative or a friend whose parents you know and trust.

■ *Don't hesitate to search for your child as soon as you discover that she or he has run away.*
Frequently, parents of runaways will convince themselves not to take action immediately but to allow their absent child a little time to let

off some steam. This strategy may be well intentioned, but it's too risky. Minute by minute, as a runaway child imagines that no one cares, her or his emotional well-being suffers. And while most runaways in this age range voluntarily return home safe and sound within twenty-four hours, the physical dangers any runaway might encounter during this time period are horrendous. Thus, it's *never* advisable to wait before trying to find your runaway child and bring her or him back home.

■ *When your child returns from running away, express your love for her or him and your pleasure that she or he is back.*
Your priority in this situation is to convince your child that returning home is in her or his best interest and to prevent her or him from turning around and running away all over again.

Remember that the typical runaway is motivated by a feeling of rejection. Reassure your child that she or he is *not* being rejected, whatever other problems both of you may be having.

■ *As much as possible, avoid punishing your child for the act of running away.*
Most likely, your child's embarrassment at having failed to remain independent and regret at having caused you so much trouble are punishment enough, although you may not see any evidence of this for a few days. Regard the incident itself as a plea for more understanding from you and act accordingly in addressing any problems or disciplinary issues that might have led to it. You may even consider having a little celebration in honor of your child's coming home.

■ *Encourage your child to have confidential relationships with other adults whom you trust.*
Children need help in understanding their parents, and the most valuable support can come from adults outside the immediate family. Far from diminishing your personal intimacy with, and authority over, your child, a close relationship between your child and another adult will actually enhance that intimacy and authority. Even more to the point, that adult will serve as a safe refuge during times when you and your child are temporarily at odds with each other so that she or he won't feel compelled simply to run away.

6.
Depression and Stress

The extra agitation of the nervous system that we call stress is inescapable for school-age children as well as for adults. In fact, a fully realized human life is inconceivable *without* it. Far from being just toxic to the emotions, making us feel frustrated, insecure, and overwrought, stress can also be a tonic—spicing life with added interest, enthusiasm, and drama.

In other words, stress in itself isn't a problem, although it may be a response to a negative situation in the environment. The real problem lies in stress *management*. And for a child in the middle years, effectively managing stress often requires parental help.

In contrast to stress, depression is an emotional illness, always characterized by feelings of hopelessness and helplessness. Like sadness, it is generally triggered by stress and, in turn, generally produces stress of its own. Unlike sadness, however, it's a psychologically paralyzed state of being that can last for several months, or longer, at a time.

Until very recently, experts assumed that depression, being much more serious in nature than sadness, could only afflict adolescents and adults, who are intellectually much more mature than children. Clinical research has since overturned this assumption. Experts now say that about 10 percent of all children suffer serious depression during their middle years—almost two-thirds the rate for adults—and that in either stage of life depression has no proven link with intellectual development. Thus, in addition to helping their school-age children control stress, parents must also be prepared to help them manage depression.

Intellectual development aside, some school-age children do seem basically more vulnerable than others to stress and, further along the stress continuum, to depression. Whether or not this quality is related to the sensitivity of their nervous systems, as some neurologists have suggested, it does seem to be constitutional in nature rather than environmental. In very deprived and abusive home (or homeless) situations and in very affluent and loving homes, the child population between the ages of six and thirteen exhibits the same spectrum of vulnerability.

At one end of this spectrum are kids who react quickly, resiliently, and resourcefully to whatever happens—good or bad. When their birthday makes them the center of attention, they're happy, poised, eager to have fun, and anxious to see that others are happy. When they receive bad news, they respond appropriately and shrug it off as best they can. When others attack them, they discharge their anger by counterattacking, but only as much as necessary to defend themselves.

At the other end of the spectrum are kids whose reaction to good or bad events is prolonged, noticeably out of proportion, and counterproductive. During their birthday celebrations, they're either very shy and embarrassed or overly excited, causing discomfort for both themselves and their guests. When bad news comes, they're either unreasonably silent or uncontrollably emotional. When they're under attack, they either withdraw immediately or counterattack with unwarranted brutality and vindictiveness.

Most school-age children are in the middle third of the spectrum—sometimes very vulnerable to stress or depression, sometimes not. That your child is more inclined to be vulnerable doesn't mean that she or he is less emotionally healthy or more emotionally disadvantaged than stronger peers. A special vulnerability to stress and depression may render an individual particularly good at fighting for justice, caring for others, appreciative of beauty, or able to foresee—and forestall—catastrophes.

No matter how your school-age child is constitutionally equipped to *receive* stress in general, you must always be ready to help your child *manage* specific incidents of stress—and, if stress should turn from bad to worse, specific incidents of depression. The best thing you can do is to make the most of every opportunity that comes along, big or small, for you and your child to enjoy each other. It not only gives your child a reservoir of happiness and high self-regard from which to draw in emergencies but also brings the two of you closer so that your child is more likely to seek help from you when it's needed.

Here are other important steps to follow:

■*Anticipate situations when your child may experience stress or depression and prepare for them accordingly.*
Certain easily foreseeable events are guaranteed to be stressful to children and may even give rise to depression as a direct consequence of the stress or as a counterbalancing aftereffect. Among such events are a stay in the hospital, the start or the end of the school year, a

scheduled visit by a relative, a planned family move, a major holiday, or the birth of a sibling. To prepare for such an event, you can begin well in advance to talk with your child so that she or he goes through it with reasonably informed expectations and to orchestrate it so that it isn't too unsettling.

Other events, equally guaranteed to be stressful, are more difficult, but still possible, to anticipate. It's all a matter of personal judgment. For example, it may or may not be appropriate to anticipate the death of a close relative who is very sick. When your child joins a ball team, it may or may not be appropriate to anticipate that she or he will not perform well.

You have less scope to prepare your child for these more hypothetical events, but you can still make sure that they don't catch him or her completely by surprise. To avoid scaring your child unnecessarily, take advantage of moments in your normal conversations to bring up such possibilities in a sensitive and constructive manner.

■ Be alert for symptoms that your child may be going through excessive stress or depression.

The universe of symptoms associated with stress and depression is basically the same. But the possible symptoms involved in a particular case of stress or depression can vary considerably from child to child.

Emotionally, these symptoms include fear, dejection, boredom, moodiness, irritability, rage, anger, or overexcitement. Behaviorally, they include any radical change in conduct, from unusual withdrawal to unusual belligerence, or from unusual placidity to unusual twitchiness and teeth clenching. Psychosomatically, they include otherwise inexplicable stomachaches, headaches, or changes in sleeping pattern or appetite.

Whether a particular constellation of symptoms indicates stress or depression is determined by how pronounced and sustained the symptoms are. In some cases, a child's symptoms may go unnoticed or ignored while they're in their "stress stage," thus increasing the odds that the child will develop a full-blown depression: a psychological condition that is much more likely to command attention.

For a school-age child experiencing stress, the symptoms usually diminish, if they don't disappear altogether, within a few days after they first appear. In severe cases of stress, they may last as long as two months; but during that period they are intermittent rather than persistent.

On the other hand, a school-age child is not clinically considered depressed until the symptoms have lasted longer than two months without significant interruption or diminution. And the extent to which the depression *might* last is entirely open-ended.

The bottom line is that stress is much less intense and much easier to treat than depression, which makes it imperative that parents do what they reasonably can to spot and alleviate the stress symptoms quickly and efficiently.

■ *Whenever your child seems troubled, be an especially good listener and observer.*
Encourage sharing of feelings by engaging your child in supportive conversations. Often children can overcome their stress or depression simply by talking it out.

A supportive conversation does not require that you judge or resolve your child's feelings. Such reactions—or their prospect—might inhibit your child from unburdening her or his soul to you. Instead, this type of conversation requires you to be especially attentive to what your child says, only offering commentary that helps her or him be more forthcoming.

During such talks, demonstrate to your child that you sympathize with an emotionally painful dilemma by *reflecting* her or his feelings. From time to time, nod affirmatively to indicate that you understand what your child is saying, paraphrase key statements, and adopt facial expressions, phrases, and vocal tones that are compatible with those that your child is using.

Reflecting your child's feelings does not mean that you condone them; rather, that you realize and appreciate the significant impact these feelings have on your child's life.

In addition to being a good listener at times when your child is overly stressed or depressed, you also need to be a good observer. Frequently the real cause of a child's emotional problems is masked—intentionally or unintentionally—by outward behavior.

For example, a child who is very upset over the loss of a parent, either through death or divorce, may subconsciously choose to be un-usually aggressive or hyperactive rather than to wallow in grief, as one might expect. Similarly, a child who is mercilessly teased about being fat by classmates may resort to abnormal overeating rather than to a more "logical" strategy of self-starvation.

When your child is behaving in a strange manner, try to observe her or him in a variety of different settings on various occasions before jumping to conclusions as to the reasons for the behavior. Also, elicit from other adults in your child's world, discreetly and confidentially, their observations.

■ *Identify what can be done to make your child feel better.*
Once you understand *how* your child is feeling and, to some degree, *why* she or he is feeling that way, solicit her or his suggestions about what can be done to alleviate these feelings or change the situation

that is causing them. Be sure to give your child some time to think about possible suggestions and ask for recommendations concerning what your child and what you—or others—can do.

If your child is unable to come up with any ideas or if those she or he voices are inappropriate, then try generating some of your own. Again, give yourself time to think about the most practical and potentially effective strategies for the particular situation at hand and include ideas concerning what your child and you or others can do.

Ideas for overcoming stress or depression tend to fall into two categories: They're either remedies or distractions. Remedies involve learning to live with, or through, the situation that is causing the stress or depression. Distractions involve diverting one's mind away from preoccupation with the cause of stress or depression. In many cases, a combination of remedies and distractions is appropriate.

For example, a child's grief for a parent who has died may be remedied (if not cured) by some sort of formal ceremony in which the child is able to say a personal good-bye to the parent: a special hour of reminiscence with the surviving parent, a gravesite visit, or a careful packing away of the deceased parent's favorite belongings. On the other hand, the same child may also be distracted from grief by going on an especially happy outing with the surviving parent, becoming involved in a new group activity, or getting a new pet.

Assuming a child is subjected to the stress of being teased about her or his weight, some remedies might be to teach the child a few good-natured "comeback" lines and to help the child follow a diet and exercise program that will trim off extra flab. Some distractions might be to lead the child to appreciate her or his admirable qualities and engage the child in activities that bolster self-esteem.

■*Avoid indirectly fostering stress and depression through overprotecting or pressuring your child.*
Children during the middle years need room to experiment with difficult life situations so that they can work out those coping strategies that best suit their individual personalities, wishes, and ambitions. It is this effort that puts them in touch with their personal genius and builds character for facing the yet more independent and complicated world of adolescence.

Although you should always be especially solicitous regarding your school-age child's emotional well-being when she or he is actually suffering from stress or depression, don't make it a habit to run interference between your child and any situation that might upset her or him. Your task as a caring parent is to *assist* your child in managing stress or depression, not to manage it yourself.

On the other hand, don't set up overly high expectations for your child regarding her or his abilities to accomplish demanding tasks, to handle difficult situations, or to meet certain standards of maturity. These expectations in themselves often cause a child to experience stress or depression.

A Timetable for Stress

Listed below are situations that are *particularly* stressful for different age groups during the middle years, although a child of *any* age during the middle years can experience *any* of the stressors cited here, regardless of the specific age group listing under which it appears.

Note that stress can result from positive situations as well as negative ones. Also note that certain individual stressors evolve and change character as a child gets older.

For example, a six- to nine-year-old's concern about rules can turn into a more sophisticated concern about responsibilities between the ages of nine and eleven. Similarly, a nine- to eleven-year-old's desire to have the same things that her or his peers have can mature into a concern about overall popularity between the ages of eleven and thirteen.

SIX TO NINE YEARS

- fighting with parents
- parents fighting with each other
- making new friends
- fighting with friends
- being teased or embarrassed
- feeling jealous and/or envious
- being ignored
- rules (remembering, obeying, or breaking)
- not getting the permission or opportunity to do things she or he feels capable of doing
- beginning school
- mother's pregnancy and/or birth or adoption of sibling
- holidays

NINE TO ELEVEN YEARS

- fighting with parents
- parents fighting with each other
- making new friends
- fighting with friends
- family move
- school tests and grades
- money and buying decisions
- games and sports
- feeling overwhelmed with responsibilities (chores, home-work, after-school activities)
- having clothes and possessions like the ones that friends have
- trying to be on time
- vacation (away from school or away from home)

ELEVEN TO THIRTEEN YEARS (EARLY ADOLESCENCE)

- family move
- change in family's standard of living (better or worse)
- parents fighting, separating, or divorcing
- school tests and grades
- money and buying decisions
- games and sports
- physical appearance
- sex-related feelings and body changes
- drugs (avoiding, choosing, or taking)
- school, community, and athletic awards, honors, and recog-nition (winning them or not)
- popularity with peers (having it or not)
- being treated, and treating others, fairly

Depression Questionnaire

The following questionnaire is adapted from instruments used by child psychiatrists and psychologists to determine whether a school-age child might be suffering from depression. It is designed to be completed by the child, but it can also be used by parents for their own rough evaluations of their child's overall emotional state.

For each numbered statement, a check is placed in the column that best describes the child's life over the past few months. A completed questionnaire with a substantial number of checks (over eight), indicating frequent negative experiences or emotions, is a possible indicator of depression.

	most times	sometimes	never
1. I like doing things now as much as I always have.			
2. I have problems sleeping.			
3. I feel sad.			
4. I have lots of energy.			
5. I enjoy being with my family.			
6. I get picked on by other kids.			
7. I feel like crying.			
8. I feel proud of what I do.			
9. I like playing with other kids.			
10. I enjoy eating at mealtimes.			
11. I feel angry.			
12. I want to get away from people.			
13. I get bored.			
14. I look forward to things now as much as I always have.			
15. I think people like me.			
16. I feel happy.			
17. I don't feel like doing things.			
18. I feel lonesome.			
19. I feel I can take care of things.			
20. I don't feel very good.			
21. I have a lot of fun.			

22. I have bad dreams.
23. I feel like giving up.
24. I enjoy my friends now as
    much as I always have.
25. I am easy to cheer up.

Coping with Family Moves

One of the most stressful and depressing events commonly faced by school-age children is a family move. In most cases, such a move involves relocating to another community and therefore a different school district. From the child's perspective, vital friendships are interrupted, reassuring routines are broken, and a beloved home base is lost.

Perhaps most disturbing of all, however, is a far more subtle issue that seldom gets acknowledged by either party in the move, the parent or the school-age child. While adjusting to the move, the school-age child must once again depend on her or his parents almost totally for emotional security, just at a stage of life when she or he was starting to develop more personal independence.

The result of this kind of setback in the child's emotional life can be a passive "giving up" to boredom, a regression to immaturity, or a rebelliousness designed to express some sort of personal power, even if it's negative. And the older the school-age child is, the worse this reaction tends to be, given the growing value a school-age child places on independence.

To make the period of transition in a family easier on the emotions of your school-age child, try following these suggestions:

■*Make sure your child knows about the move—and the reasons behind the move—well in advance of the moving day.*

The earlier your child is told about the move, the more time to adjust to the change. And the more carefully you explain all the positive reasons for moving, the easier it will be for your child to think of the change as desirable.

Be specific about the time and circumstances surrounding the actual moving day so that it comes across to your child as a well-planned, easily envisioned, and inevitable event. Also, include among your announced reasons for moving specific factors that can appeal to your child: for example, a larger bedroom, a bedroom of her or his own, a bigger yard for playing, a better school, closer proximity to favorite relatives or to favorite recreational areas.

Don't be disappointed if your child doesn't mirror your enthusiasm for the move right away. What's important is not that your child is "sold" on the move but that she or he has some attractive images to ponder that are directly associated with the move.

■ *Acknowledge the difficulties associated with the move and indicate your faith that they will be overcome.*
Your child needs to know that you understand what a shock the move might be to her or his personal universe. Allow her or him to express freely and fully any anxious feelings about the move and indicate that they are natural, given the circumstances. Then make it clear to your child that you'll do whatever you can to make the move more positive and that you have confidence in her or his coping abilities and future happiness.

■ *Involve your child in learning more about where you are going to move.*
Share maps, photographs, newspapers, and stories with your child that will foster a familiarity with your new place of residence. If possible, make numerous visits there in advance of moving day so that she or he can begin to develop favorite sights and experiences associated with your new home.

■ *Give your child special tasks during the move.*
Put your child in charge of certain age-appropriate aspects of the move, such as packing and labeling all the household tools, finding sturdy boxes in the neighborhood, compiling a list of all the people to whom to say good-bye, or unpacking certain specific boxes in the new home. These responsibilities will help your child feel more as if she or he is helping to make the move happen.

■ *Once you've moved into your new home, get involved with your child in family-oriented activities sponsored by the school, the community, or local organizations.*
In doing so, you will not only be exposing your child to potential new friends and pleasurable pastimes, you will also be setting an example for your child of how to enter into a new situation

and make the most of it. Start by checking out the PTA, scouting organizations, church or synagogue groups, and lists of family-oriented activities in local newspapers.

Coping with Serious Illness

School-age children who have a chronic health problem, such as asthma, epilepsy, diabetes, or sickle-cell anemia, or who are suffering from a long-term illness, such as severe mononucleosis, nerve paralysis, hepatitis, or leukemia, have special emotional needs. Besides worrying more than their peers about their physical well-being, they must also go through the psychological turmoil associated with not being able to live a fuller life, like their healthier peers.

A younger child during the middle years often subconsciously assumes that her or his illness is some sort of punishment for being bad. An older child during the same period tends to be angry with her or his parents and physicians for not being able to deal with the illness more successfully. And a child of any age during the middle years is likely to experience despair, a lack of self-confidence, and mixed feelings of attraction and repulsion toward being pampered or being paid any sort of attention at all.

You can help your child cope with stress, depression, and other emotional turmoil that can accompany a serious illness by doing the following things:

■ *Make sure both you and your child are as well informed as possible about the illness and what it means.*

Ask your child's medical-care team for full information about her or his condition, including detailed directions regarding what your child can do, should do, and should not do given the condition. Stick to professional judgments in deciding what rules will govern your child's behavior and daily life, taking care not to be either excessively cautious or permissive. It's also a good idea to read about your child's condition in reputable medical books and to talk about the condition with others—doctors, parents, or victims—who are informed about that condition. However, it is *not* a good idea to take for granted anything you read or hear about your child's condition from someone who is not closely involved in her or his treatment.

Always bear in mind that each case of a serious illness is different. Before you act on anything you read or hear about your child's condition, verify it with her or his medical team.

■ *Avoid making your child feel vulnerable or exceptional.*
The more your child is able to feel competent and normal, the more positive her or his self-image will be and, therefore, the greater her or his sense of emotional security. Refer to your child's medical problems only when absolutely necessary. Otherwise, remain focused on her or his strengths as an individual and her or his natural and social evolution as a school-age kid.

■ *Encourage your child to engage in activities that will develop self-confidence and self-esteem.*
School-age children with serious illnesses frequently have a lot of "rest time" on their hands. Guide your child in using such time constructively by turning her or his interests and talents into hobbies and skills.

Also, seek opportunities for your child to enjoy and display skill mastery in the company of others. Depending on your child's particular skills and the nature of the illness, appropriate opportunities may include participating on athletic teams, in game or hobby clubs, in school or fair competitions, in choirs, bands, or orchestras, or in informal play sessions with other children.

■ *Get outside support for both you and your child.*
If your child's illness is serious, then it's important to line up people to whom you can turn for help in a crisis. Check out local support groups both for victims of illness and for their families.

Consider going to a family-oriented psychiatrist or psychologist for an evaluation of your child's emotional response to being ill. This initial contact can pave the way for future help whenever you and/or your child are experiencing difficulties in coping with the illness.

At PCGC: Seasonal Affective Disorder

Seasonal affective disorder, or SAD, is a form of depression that is attributed to seasonal changes in natural light, as registered on the retina and processed in the brain. Other factors, such as wintertime temperature and humidity changes, may also be involved in SAD, but less is known about how they might operate. Also, some people experience decreased alertness, increased sleepiness, and sustained depression in *summer* instead of winter, a condition called reverse SAD. This latter condition, far less prevalent than SAD itself, may be related to a latent summer-hibernation drive in the victim's brain, like the one that is activated in many animals during hot and dry seasons.

Most people barely register *any* major, season-related changes in their emotional state aside from holiday-related ups and downs or occasional bouts of "spring fever." However, many live throughout each winter with noticeably strong symptoms of depression, including children as young as six years old (so far the earliest age at which SAD symptoms have been clinically detectable).

The Mood, Sleep, and Seasonality Program at PCGC studies how child and adolescent depression relates to the seasons and what long-term effects such depression may have on its sufferers. The program has established that adolescents with SAD regularly exhibit various combinations of the following symptoms during the winter months:

■ extreme tiredness and listlessness;

■ appetite changes: most often an *increase* in appetite (possibly as the result of winter-triggered carbohydrate-craving obesity syndrome [COS]);

■ frequent irritability and negativity;

■ persistent and pronounced sadness;

■ difficulty in concentrating, often accompanied by a slowness in thinking and causing a downward trend in school performance;

■ sleep changes: either too much or too little;

■ withdrawal from family and peer social activities.

According to what the Mood, Sleep, and Seasonality Program has learned to date, school-age SAD is typically not as intense as adolescent SAD, which, in turn, is inclined to be less severe than adult SAD. The implication is that an untreated case of SAD worsens over time and that early intervention—especially if it occurs during the victim's middle childhood—can make a significant difference in the victim's lifelong emotional state.

A child is referred to PCGC's Mood, Sleep, and Seasonality Program by her or his parents and/or teachers. A psychiatrist then assesses the various biological, psychological, environmental, and family elements that may be contributing to the child's apparently season-related depression. One such element may be heredity. Both SAD and other forms of extreme seasonal mood and energy variation tend to occur in family groups; and family members from different generations may go through persistent seasonal mood changes of differing intensities.

Ultimately, the program psychiatrist arrives at a specific diagnosis, which may point to season-related depression but not SAD itself. Then the psychiatrist outlines a treatment plan tailored to the particular needs of the child and family.

Among the most successful treatments for SAD is phototherapy, which involves daily exposure for approximately an hour or more (depending on the case) to banks of high-intensity light. This type of exposure has worked to counteract many of the effects of SAD in approximately 80 percent of the patients admitted to the program.

If you have reason to believe that SAD may be affecting your school-age child, discuss the possibility with your psychiatrist, psychologist, or mental-health professional. She or he may be able to arrange for diagnosis and treatment.

At PCGC: Pain Management for School-Age Children

Compared to all that we know about the emotional and physiological factors relating to *adult* pain, there is a surprising lack of information and education about the emotional and physiological factors relating to *children*'s pain. As a result, many misconceptions exist, such as the false notions that children do not feel pain as intensely as adults and that they are essentially incapable of managing the pain they do feel.

The best way for hospitals and clinics to help child patients and their families cope more intelligently with severe or chronic pain is to coordinate medical, psychological, nursing, physical therapy, and technological resources into an integrated treatment plan. Increasingly, hospitals and clinics are aiming in this direction.

The guiding philosophy of this kind of "pain management" is to minimize the child's pain as much as possible while at the same time increasing her or his ability to function. For example, in the Pain Management Program conducted by The Children's Hospital of Philadelphia and PCGC, a so-called pain management team of professionals is assigned to each case. To treat the physical aspects of pain, physicians on these teams rely on new medications, old medications used in new ways, and innovative techniques in administering medications. To address the psychological aspects of pain, psychiatrists and psychologists on these teams rely on various nonmedical methods to help the child cope with pain and the family manage stress factors associated with it. Among these nonmedical methods are the following:

ACTIVE LISTENING

Children in pain often feel that other pepole—especially adults—are incapable of understanding or appreciating what they are going through. Team members always exercise active listening skills when they are working with a child, and they teach family members and caretakers to do the same. The main active listening skills are as follows:

■ establishing trust with the child;

■ encouraging the child to talk openly about painful experiences;

■ not interrupting or "speaking for" the child;

■ never questioning what the child says about her or his pain;

■ demonstrating that you understand and respect what the child has said.

BIOFEEDBACK

Using a computer, child patients are able to see or hear their own physiological reaction to pain. This helps them put the pain into a more realistic perspective and inspires them to work effectively toward reducing it.

For example, a girl with chronic leg pain can attach computer-connected electrodes to her leg and then engage in relaxation techniques aimed at easing her leg pain. As these techniques change the level of her skin conductivity, thus indicating a relaxation of her leg pain, she sees the change registered by the computer: A train appears on the screen and runs downhill on a track. Through this kind of activity she learns to direct her attention more and more toward *controlling* her physiological reactions instead of just *expressing* her discomfort.

SELF-HYPNOSIS AND RELAXATION

Many techniques exist for teaching a child how to relax, including deep muscle relaxation or visual imagery. The techniques chosen for a specific case depend on the age of the patient and the nature of the pain.

Take, for instance, the relatively extreme case of a boy with cancer who is frightened of bone-marrow aspirations. His anxiety makes the procedure even more painful than it normally is. To alleviate the anxiety, the boy can be taught to visualize a line running from the back of his neck to the place on his body where he feels the pain and then to imagine that he himself is turning the wire on and off. Eventually, he can learn to "let go" of his pain when the wire is "off" and thereby tolerate the temporary procedure with much less discomfort.

PAIN DIARY

A pain diary is a written account—often supplemented with drawings, charts, or graphs—of when and where the pain occurs, what seems to precipitate the pain, and how intense the pain is (e.g., on a "pain is . . ." scale of "slight," "bad," "very bad," or "awful"). By helping a child keep such an account, family members can assist themselves and their child in gaining a more tangible understanding of the pain and thereby have more control over pain-related experiences.

FAMILY COUNSELING

Counseling for some or all of the child's family members can help ease ongoing or intermittent tensions that may be contributing to the child's pain. In addition, such counseling can teach family members how to cope with the personal and interpersonal difficulties caused specifically by the illness as well as how to assist the child in coping more effectively with the pain, given the overall family situation at hand.

Look for hospitals or clinics in your area that provide pain management programs similar to the program described above. If none is available, consult your physician or mental-health professional about creating a similar kind of treatment plan for your child.

7.
Lying and Stealing

Children over the age of six are definitely old enough to know when they are lying or stealing and, what's more important, that both are wrong. Nevertheless, even the most well behaved and morally sensitive child may occasionally resort to such behavior. The possible rationales for it during a child's middle years are numerous; and the tendency toward rationalization during these years is very strong and can easily turn irresistible, depending on the circumstances.

Among the major reasons why a school-age child is tempted to lie or steal are the following:

■ The child is trying to get even for a perceived injustice. For example, she or he may steal a sibling's prized possession upon feeling that the latter has been unfairly overbearing, or circulate a vicious lie about a friend if she or he feels betrayed by that friend.

■ The child is trying to avoid something undesirable. For example, a sick child may lie and feign illness in order to prevent having to put up with an unwanted therapy, or a child may steal money rather than go through the humiliating ordeal of begging for it and then lie in order to escape punishment.

■ The child is testing people for their reactions. For example, a child may tell a teacher lies about her or his home life in order to learn more about the latter's capacity to be fooled or attitude toward a certain issue (the subject of the lie). Or the child may steal a playmate's hat just to see how she or he behaves without it.

■ The child is attempting to prove her or his daring. For example, a child may steal a garden tool from a garage simply to prove that she or he isn't really afraid of an intimidating neighbor, or may lie in the presence of other kids who know the truth simply to impress them with her or his bravado.

■ The child is trying to get more attention. For example, a child may steal a bracelet her or his mother is sure to miss as an indirect means of forcing some sort of interaction with her, even if it is negative, or may lie about being ill in order to elicit more hands-on care and sympathy.

Assuming you handle your school-age child's early episodes of lying or stealing in a forthright, loving, and effective manner, she or he should outgrow this type of behavior fairly quickly. Try following these guidelines:

■ *Be sure that you and your child agree that lying and stealing are not to be tolerated.*

It's one thing for your child to realize that lying and stealing are wrong; it's quite another for her or him to understand *why* these activities are wrong and to make a personal commitment not to lie or steal based on that understanding.

In addition to reminding your child from time to time, directly or indirectly, that you disapprove of lying and stealing, ascertain whether she or he also does. Also, probe, when appropriate, to make certain that your child appreciates *why* lying and stealing are wrong.

■ *Take any instance of lying and stealing seriously.*

You shouldn't berate or punish your child too severely for lying or stealing, because occasional incidents of this kind of behavior are to be expected in this age range. At the same time, you shouldn't let an instance of it pass unmentioned or—even worse—be treated as a harmless prank.

Discuss every case of lying or stealing with your child as it comes to your attention, being careful not to criticize your child her- or himself but rather what she or he did. Give your child a full opportunity to account for any wrongdoing and guide her or him toward appreciating the gravity of the matter.

■ *Help your child figure out more acceptable ways she or he might have behaved instead of resorting to lying or stealing.*

Often children lie or steal because they can't think of any other way to behave in order to achieve their desired goal. For example, a child may lie to a relative in order to avoid having to spend time alone with her or him. Try role-playing such situations with your child so that she or he can learn more acceptable behaviors.

■ *Cooperate with your child to work out any restitution for the lie or the theft.*

Your child should assume responsibility for her or his wrongdoings and do whatever possible to make up for them, but this doesn't mean you can't help. For example, don't hesitate to accompany your child on an apology mission if she or he asks you to do so, and consider helping your child replace any object that she or he has stolen if doing so all alone would be particularly difficult.

■ *Never allow your child to profit from lying or stealing.*
Insist that your child forgo any advantage gained—directly or indirectly—as a result of the lie or the theft. Under no circumstances should you allow your child to "get away" with a lie if it's at all possible to correct it with the truth, nor should you allow a stolen object to be kept.

■ *Avoid harsh punishments for lying or stealing and don't suggest to your child that you no longer trust her or him.*
In cases when the lie or the theft is not very damaging, you should be fairly quick to forgive. If a child is made to appreciate the wrongness of what she or he has done and also makes restitution for the lie or the theft, she or he should not have to go through any further punishment. In cases of especially damaging lies or thefts, you might want to add some temporary, mild form of punishment simply to underscore the seriousness of the incident.

Whatever the situation, never permit your child to feel that the damage is irreparable or that she or he will forever suffer the consequences of having lied or stolen. You don't want your child to give up trying to be good or to develop such a bad self-image that she or he starts having serious emotional problems.

CASE:

A Plea to Play

Carl begged his parents to let him join the neighborhood touch football team, but they refused. At nine years old, Carl would have been the youngest member of the team, which consisted of ten- and eleven-year-olds, and his parents were concerned that he might get hurt. A very obedient son, Carl was forced to accept their judgment, albeit not with the best of spirits.

It was shortly afterward that Carl's parents first began missing some of their personal possessions. His father somehow lost or misplaced his harmonica. The crystal swan that usually sat on his mother's bureau suddenly disappeared. One day, when his mother made a rare trip to the attic to look for an old photo album, she discovered the two objects and several other stolen items of little practical value tucked away in a battered old suitcase. She knew only Carl could have taken them.

When she confronted Carl about her discovery, he at first denied stealing the objects, but he eventually broke down and confessed. He apologized profusely and swore to his mother that he had just taken the objects because he liked them so much and wanted to have them all to himself. He seemed so contrite that his mother accepted his account and forgave him, even though she remained perplexed about why such a basically good child would suddenly resort to stealing.

Later, Carl's fourth-grade teacher called his mother in for a special conference and informed her that Carl had been caught stealing small, fairly insignificant items from her desk and from those of some of the other students. Distraught, his mother told his teacher about the thefts at home. His teacher then asked, "Has Carl been upset about anything lately? Is there any reason that he might be feeling unhappy, or angry, or lost?"

Carl's mother recalled the time that Carl had been so disappointed at not being allowed to play football with the other boys in the neighborhood. Convinced that Carl's frustration over this decision—one with which he had been unable, rationally and emotionally, to agree—might be driving him to retaliate by stealing, his teacher suggested that his parents talk with the school athletic director about the appropriateness of letting Carl play on the team.

After the athletic director, well acquainted with Carl and his physical capabilities, advised Carl's parents that it would be all right for him to play with the team, they gave their permission. Carl was overjoyed, and no further incidents of stealing occurred.

8.
Sibling Rivalry

Tensions, arguments, and outright fights between siblings are inevitable, no matter how mild mannered or basically compatible the two individuals may be. In fact, two siblings involved in a "normal" relationship may spend up to half their time in conflict with one another. It is part of a necessarily slow and complex process of learning how to get along together in a polite, responsible, and mutually satisfying manner.

The phrase "sibling rivalry" refers to especially significant contests of will that occur during this process. Rivalry situations stand out from others that are conflict-related not only because they tend to be more intense but also because they so often serve as contexts for a child to express more deep-seated emotional needs that may or may not have anything to do with a sibling.

On the surface, a child engaged in a rivalry struggle with a sibling is vying with that sibling for a specific right, honor, power, or possession. Beneath the surface, however, the child may be seeking more parental attention, acting out anger at a friend, or trying to compensate for a failure at school. Dealing effectively as a parent with sibling rivalry demands being sensitive both to surface issues and to possible underlying issues.

Sibling-rivalry situations occur most frequently with a child between the ages of six and nine. They typically involve fights relating to dominance (e.g., determining who gets to set the rules for a game) or to the possession, division, or sharing of tangible items (e.g., determining who gets to play with the video games).

A younger sibling within this age range typically initiates a rivalry battle indirectly by teasing or aggravating an older sibling into open retaliation. An older child within this age range typically provokes a rivalry battle by "bossing" a younger sibling beyond the usual limits that are more or less accepted by both of them.

Between the ages of nine and thirteen, sibling-rivalry contests are usually much less frequent and much less bothersome, although rivalry in itself can still be a major factor in the relationship between two siblings. Rivalry battles within this age range commonly relate to more intangible issues, such as recognition (e.g., establishing who performs a certain skill better) or fairness (e.g., determining whether one sibling's rights, privileges, and responsibilities are appropriate in comparison with those of another sibling).

Whether or not two siblings are two brothers, two sisters, or brother and sister doesn't appear to make much difference in the quality or frequency of their sibling-rivalry contests. However, sibling rivalry between a brother and a sister can take on a gender-related dimension. A brother, for example, may justly or unjustly accuse his sister of receiving kinder treatment simply because she's a girl, or a sister may justly or unjustly accuse her brother of being allowed more freedom simply because he's a boy. Parents faced with this kind of dilemma need to examine carefully whether their own parenting style or behavior as individuals may be partly responsible for such accusations. If it appears that this may be true, then the parents need to amend their parenting style or their behavior as individuals so that it is less conducive to sexism.

Here are some other tips for parents who need help in managing sibling rivalry:

■ *Try to give each child a similar amount of attention.*

Bear in mind that one of the most potent catalysts of sibling rivalry is a desire to attract parental attention. Take care to spend time individually with each of your children on a frequent, regular, and dependable basis.

Giving your children a *similar* amount of individual attention does not necessarily mean always giving them an *equal* amount. Although equality of attention is an ideal goal, there are certain specific circumstances or occasions that warrant giving one child more attention than another.

For example, if one child is seriously ill physically or emotionally, most of the parents' available time may rightfully have to be spent caring for her or him. In such a case, the parents should explain the circumstances to each other child and continue to give each one some amount of individual attention every day, even if it's only for a few moments. Then, at the earliest possible opportunity, the parents should do something special with each other child individually.

Another example of a time when strict equality of individual attention is not appropriate is a child's birthday. On this day, the birthday celebrant should definitely be the center of attention, but the parents should also make the day special for the other children by involving them in the celebration plans and activities and by giving them small gifts as reminders that they, too, are loved and remembered.

■ *Give clear guidelines to all your children regarding each child's respective possessions, privileges, and rights.*
Make sure that every child knows who "owns" what, who is entitled to which age-appropriate privileges, and what rights each child has in common with the others (such as the right of privacy). As much as possible, make such declarations in the presence of all your children so that there is no chance for one child to plead ignorance to another.

Also, let your children know how you expect them to interact with each other. Tell them, for example, that you do not want any physical abuse or name-calling.

■ *Don't compare one child to another.*
As much as possible, avoid making statements to your child like "Why aren't you as nice to your grandmother as your brother is?" or "If your sister can get ready for school all by herself, so can you." Also, avoid letting your child overhear you saying to someone else things like "Robert was a real quiet baby, but Mac was a terror" or "Jamie has the looks, and Wendy has the brains." These kinds of comparisons can easily give rise to taunts and resentment between children. Instead, help your children appreciate their differences in a noncompetitive manner.

■ *As much as possible, allow your child to settle their own conflicts.*
One of the most troublesome and unsavory aspects of sibling rivalry is tattling, which usually puts a parent in the position of taking one child's side against another without the benefit of knowing what really happened. As much as possible, resist cooperating with the tattler. Instead, make it clear that you expect your children to work out their own differences.

In order to assist your children in handling their rivalry conflicts, take every opportunity to teach them good problem-solving strategies. Any such strategy should include both children first taking a moment or two to cool down and then reasoning out a decision that is mutually satisfactory.

Of course, school-age children are not always capable of reasoning out problems they have with their siblings, so you have to be prepared to allow a certain percentage of them to remain unresolved for an indefinite period of time. Try to intervene only when they are clearly undermining a child's emotional health or the proper functioning of family life.

■ *Encourage positive sibling interactions.*

Guide your children toward playing cooperatively, in a manner that is appropriate to their respective ages. Remember that a child is generally not ready for roughhouse games or strongly competitive games until around age eight.

Try involving your children in performing chores cooperatively. This might help them learn to have more patience with each other and to appreciate each other's capabilities and limitations. When your children work especially well together in accomplishing a certain task, be sure to praise them for their cooperation.

Meanwhile, periodically engage your children in activities that they can enjoy in each other's company, such as camping trips or visits to the zoo. Shared memories of good times make powerful bonds between siblings.

Finally, reinforce those moments when your children demonstrate love for each other. A younger child often feels very proud of an older sibling, and an older one often feels very protective toward a younger one. Subtly support such feelings and make them more memorable for both children.

■ *Encourage each child to develop an independent life.*

One of the best ways to reduce the frequency and intensity of sibling-rivalry situations is to make it possible for each child to have a personally rewarding life of her or his own. Help each child realize her or his own interests and talents. Then give each one time and space for cultivating those talents and interests and insist that your other children do the same.

CASE:

Putting a Stop to Fights

Nine-year-old Cassie and seven-year-old Warren bickered, argued, or fought together almost every day. Concerned about the frequency of this type of behavior, their parents secretly kept track of when, where, how, and why it occurred over a period of two weeks.

The parents discovered that Cassie and Warren most often quarreled at times when both parents were nearby and that these particular squabbles inevitably featured screaming and/ or other loud noises as well as "stagy" pleas for justice. It seemed clear to the parents that the children were fighting in order to get their attention. Sure enough, when the parents paid them no heed at such times and instead gave them more consideration when they behaved well, the incidence of fighting dropped considerably.

Nevertheless, during long car trips Cassie and Warren would still wind up fighting. It was as if they knew that their parents were a captive audience in such a situation. Finally, the parents hit upon a solution. Before the next long car trip, they told their kids that they would stop the car if the kids started quarreling.

After an hour of traveling, Warren and Cassie began fighting, and their father, who was driving at the time, pulled over to the side of the road and parked. He gave no reason for doing so; he simply waited until the kids quieted down. Then he started up again. Rarely again did he ever have to stop during a car trip.

9.
Divorce

At its very best, divorce is still traumatic. And it's especially so for children during the middle years. Having outgrown the almost total self-centeredness of the preschool years, kids between the ages of six and thirteen increasingly identify with their parents, relying on them for their own sense of self and turning to them as models of rational, adult behavior. Thus, a breakup of their parents' marriage throws their whole world and their whole future development as individuals into doubt.

To add to this trauma, a school-age child is just learning to be independent from home life, a condition thrust upon the child when her or his formal schooling began. The threat to home life implicit in any divorce disturbs this learning process. Suddenly, the child reverts to a longing for the stable, all-nourishing home environment she or he knew as an infant and suffers pangs of anger, fear, and resentment that such an environment no longer exists. The child may even feel guilt about having contributed to the dissolution of the family by having "left home" for school.

If you are contemplating a divorce or going through one, consider these ways to prevent, alleviate, or resolve much of that doubt for your child:

■ *Don't pretend that the divorce is "good" and don't expect your child to appreciate your rationale for the divorce.*
A divorce needs to be presented to school-age children as a fact of life—a firm and final decision that has been made by the two adults involved. Therefore, guard against talking to your school-age child about the possibility of a divorce. Instead, wait until divorce is a certainty and then announce it to your child as soon as you reasonably can—preferably together with your spouse.

From the child's point of view, a divorce can't help but seem like a negative development. With this in mind, don't confuse your child or discredit her or his sorrowful feelings by trying to convince her or him that your divorce is a positive development. Acknowledge that the divorce is bad news but that you're hoping that all of you will try to get through it as best you can.

Also, don't express your reasons for the divorce as if it were something that was strictly a logical matter, that is, something that you could conceivably be reasoned out of doing. Instead, describe the divorce as the only alternative you have given the fact that the two of you have too many irreconcilable differences and are no longer able to live with each other.

■ *Avoid assigning blame for the divorce or criticizing the other party in your child's presence.*

Beyond any other consideration, your child needs to maintain positive images of both parents in order to feel good about her- or himself. Resist the temptation to "expose" the other parent's character flaws or misbehavior to your child or to vent your anger or disappointment on the other parent in conversations with your child.

It may be necessary to inform your child about unpleasant facts leading to the divorce decision. For example, you or your spouse may have developed another, very serious romantic relationship or created serious legal or financial problems that made the marriage no longer tenable. Giving your child this information may be the only way you can spare her or him the pain of learning these facts later in a negative way or the feeling of having been deceived once the facts become known.

If it is necessary to communicate unpleasant facts that led to your divorce decision, present them as calmly and simply as you can. Remember always to cast disapproval on the deed, not the person.

■ *Reassure your child that she or he did not cause the divorce and will continue to be loved and tended by both parents.*

Frequently remind your child of these facts during the transition process. Also, try to give your child more specific images of *how* she or he will receive each parent's love and attention in the future: for example, when, how, and how often she or he will be in contact with the noncustodial parent.

Also, the more you and your divorcing partner can join together in doing things with your child—before, during, and after the divorce— the better. It helps convince your child that her or his welfare can transcend the individual differences her or his parents have. Just make sure that these occasions of togetherness can and do take place without any outbreaks of open hostility. Also, be careful not to feed your child's wish that you and your divorcing partner might get back together sometime in the future.

■*Don't put your child on the spot by involving her or him in divorce-related decisions.*

Your child shouldn't be forced, directly or indirectly, to choose one parent over the other. This type of decision making inevitably results in loyalty conflicts that could cause long-term emotional problems for your child.

With your child's welfare uppermost in your minds and with the understanding that she or he needs both parents actively involved in her or his life, you and your divorcing partner should make all decisions relating to child custody, child visitation, and division of parenting responsibilities. Don't turn your child into a consultant, judge, or jury.

■*Keep your child informed about divorce-related events and decisions in a timely and frank manner.*

One of the worst fears a school-age child can have about a divorce is to feel left out of the event entirely. Talk with your child at regular intervals during the divorce process about what has happened, what's happening currently, and what's going to happen.

In these talks, try to remain fairly calm, but don't be afraid to let your child know—very briefly and undramatically—that you yourself are worried, depressed, or confused. It prepares your child for moments when you won't be functioning quite as smoothly as before, and it may create an opportunity to talk about her or his own divorce-related emotional problems.

■*As much as possible, avoid making changes in your child's normal routines.*

The more your child's day-to-day life remains familiar, comfortable, and predictable, the more reassured she or he will be about the safety and happiness of life in the future, despite the divorce. Try to put off making any major changes in your child's life, whether they are divorce related or not, until after she or he has had at least a few months to adjust to the divorce itself.

■*Allow your child full freedom to express her or his feelings both to you and to other trusted adults.*

Always make time to ask your child how she or he is doing from time to time during the divorce process and to listen nonjudgmentally to your child's fears, worries, grievances, and complaints. However, don't pressure your child to communicate if she or he isn't forthcoming. In many divorce situations, children simply don't have much to say, and you don't want to scare or depress them unnecessarily.

It can also be very helpful for school-age children to be able to discuss the divorce with other adults—relatives and friends who can be trusted to be honest, fair, and reassuring. Tactfully encourage such discussions by arranging for your child to have some time alone with adults you trust. Just be sure to prepare the adults for these talks. Keep them informed about the divorce itself so that they won't be inclined to pump your child for information, and give them guidelines for talking about divorce-related issues so that they won't, for example, wind up casting blame on anyone or setting up false expectations.

Helping Kids Handle Parental Dating and Remarriage

There are three main reasons why school-age children are very likely to have difficulties accepting the romantic lives of their divorced parents.

1. Children between the ages of six and thirteen are typically not mature enough to appreciate the need of adults for peer companionship, much less their desire for sexual gratification.

2. They are typically too dependent on their parents' time and energy not to feel that it's a sacrifice to allow their parents the personal freedom for a romantic life.

3. They are typically identifying with their parents very strongly and can therefore easily be disturbed by aspects of their parents' lives that they cannot—and often don't want to—share.

If you are a divorced parent of a school-age child and are concerned about the emotional effects on your child of your dating or remarrying, here are some guidelines for making such situations more pleasurable for all parties involved:

■ *Wait until you know your new romantic interest fairly well before arranging for her or him and your child to spend time together.*

You don't have to go out of your way to avoid any meeting at all between the person you are dating and your child. However, it is a good idea not to throw them together socially until you yourself are comfortable with your date and have a reasonably well informed idea of how your date and your child will get along.

Above all, avoid leaving your child alone with your date until you know her or him very well and until after you, your date, and your child have spent time together on numerous occasions. Your child may feel very shy and awkward at being left alone with your date while she or he is still a comparative stranger, and this shyness or awkwardness can easily translate into displeasure or even fear.

■ *Allow your child to get used to this person gradually, at her or his own pace.*

Avoid communicating—or even forming—high expectations about how your child and your date will respond to each other. School-age children are typically very guarded in forming a new relationship with an adult; and as such a relationship develops, they often resort to brief periods of false behavior—for example, mock flirtation or mock rejection—in order to try out their new acquaintance's reactions.

As a parent, you need to respond to your child's *apparent* feelings about your date in a calm and constructive manner. Just don't jump to conclusions about her or his *true* feelings regarding your date. Be patient and allow them to emerge in their own way and their own time.

Part of being patient is allowing your child certain emotionally important freedoms. Don't insist that your child be friends with your date, act a certain way, or call your date by a certain name. And continue to allow your child this freedom even if your date ultimately becomes your child's stepparent.

■ *Keep your child informed about your relationship but don't force your child to make decisions about it.*

While your child will definitely appreciate your sharing basic information about your ongoing romantic relationships (information that's appropriate to her or his age as a listener), it won't make your child feel important if you ask for permission to date or marry someone. It will simply add to her or his anxiety about the situation. Be responsible to yourself and your family for your own romantic relationships and respect the fact that your child is your dependent, not your partner.

■ *Involve your child in your marriage plans in an appropriate manner.*

Announce your marriage intentions to your child as soon as possible and make sure that there is a sufficient "adjustment time" between this announcement and the wedding—at least a month. Then give your child mutually agreeable roles to play in preparing for and participating in the wedding and making any physical arrangements necessary for setting up a new household.

During the weeks immediately before and after the wedding, take care to maintain regular, dependable hours of private time for just you and your child. This will help ensure that your child doesn't feel as if she or he were losing you to your new spouse. Also, reserve a similar amount of private time for just you and your partner so that she or he won't feel slighted by the attention you pay your child. The honeymoon itself, for example, should definitely *not* include your child, even if this means postponing it until arrangements can be made for your child's care while you are away.

■ *Seek agreement with your new spouse on child-rearing policies.*

Coordinating with your spouse ahead of time on child-rearing policies reduces the odds that your child will be distressed by parental quarrels in her or his name or different messages from each parent. As much as possible, your child-rearing policies should be the same *after* your marriage as they were *before* so that your child can feel more comfortable with this new phase of family life.

10.
The Adopted Child

The earlier a child is told that she or he is adopted, the better. Parents can begin to refer to their child's adopted status from the moment they begin talking to their child, in casual remarks like "I'm so glad we adopted you!" As their child matures, so can the references to the adoption.

If, instead, parents withhold this vital piece of information for any length of time at all, the child may view the adoption as a shameful thing when she or he is finally told about it. Otherwise, she or he may reason, why was the adoption kept a secret?

Unfortunately, many parents do put off telling their child that she or he is adopted until she or he has reached school age. Because their child is then considered "just old enough" for formal education, these parents apparently assume that she or he is also "just old enough" to understand what "adopted" really means.

In fact, waiting until a child is of school age to talk about her or his adopted status is *not* advisable. Far from being the best time for a child to deal with the fact that she or he was adopted, the middle years are perhaps the worst.

From all the evidence we have, preschoolers remain fairly untroubled by the knowledge that they were adopted. During the years between six and thirteen, however, the situation can be very different. Children who have known about their adopted status since babyhood are inclined to be much more bothered by it during this age span. And children who are just learning about their adopted status during this age period are inclined to be even more upset.

Researchers testing both adopted and biological children of all ages are unable to distinguish one group from the other psychologically until around the age of six, at which point adopted children as a group do begin showing more signs of emotional trouble than do biological children. Common symptoms of such trouble include depression, withdrawal, aggression, hyperactivity, and/or defiance, and they remain noticeably more prevalent among adopted children than biological children until adolescence, when the two groups of children again become less psychologically distinguishable.

Why should concern about having been adopted manifest itself so much more strongly during a child's middle years than during the early years of adolescence? There are three basic reasons for this phenomenon:

1. Compared to the average preschooler, the average school-age child has much more peer contact and is therefore much more distressed about being different. The adopted school-age child is keenly aware that most peers live with their biological parents, and her or his imagination may very well interpret this difference as being far more significant than it actually is.

By adolescence, the school-age child is less likely to read as much meaning into the difference. She or he may still want to resemble her or his most valued peers, but this desire for resemblance is less involved with the family relationships of those peers.

2. The average school-age child is just learning to view the world rationally and logically, and so the adopted school-age child is inevitably led to speculate about *why* she or he was put up for adoption. Among the questions that typically torment such a child are the following:

■ Was I rejected because I wasn't sufficiently smart or attractive?

■ Were my real parents evil or careless people who wanted nothing to do with raising a child?

■ Was the adoption itself the tragic result of an accident, a misunderstanding, or even a crime?

These kinds of speculation can stir up intense feelings of abandonment, grief, loneliness, resentment, and guilt—feelings that are easier for an adolescent to ignore, manage, or overcome.

3. School-age children are deeply involved in establishing more mature, person-to-person relationships with their parents. They identify with them, imitate them, test personal differences against them, bargain with them, and seek common ground with them.

These activities are much more problematic for a school-age child who is adopted. The adopted child can always attribute incompatibilities with her or his parents to the fact that she or he is not their biological child, and such incompatibilities inevitably seem more threatening and more difficult to resolve.

By the time adopted children are teenagers, they, like most teenagers, are not so bothered about being different from their parents.

They're more concerned about person-to-person relationships with their peers. When they do show concern about their biological parents versus their adoptive ones, it's usually a matter of curiosity. They may want to know the identity of their biological parents or even to track them down; but this desire is more intellectual than emotional in nature.

This doesn't preclude the fact that some adopted children have a lifelong and deep-seated longing to find out about, or reconnect with, their biological parents. As a rule, however, such children will express this desire in relatively plain terms to their adopted parents.

If you have not yet told your school-age child that she or he is adopted, then by all means do so as soon and as positively as possible. Unfortunate as the timing may be, it is better for your child to know about her or his adopted status sooner rather than later.

Make a special, private occasion out of the announcement and explain your delay in telling your child about the adoption in terms of your wish to demonstrate your own parental love during her or his early years, *not* in terms of her or his inability during those years to understand or accept the news.

Whether or not you have waited to tell your child about being adopted, here are some ways to help her or him deal with her or his adopted status during the especially sensitive middle years of childhood:

■ *Always refer to the adoption itself, and to the status of being an adopted child, in positive terms.*

Whatever you know—or don't know—about the circumstances leading to your child's availability for adoption, reassure your child that she or he was loved by her or his biological parents and that they were doing what they thought was best for her or his welfare. Also, describe your first meeting with your child in loving detail, emphasizing the pleasure that you felt and that your child expressed.

In regard to the status of being adopted, make sure your child realizes that your decision to adopt her or him came from the heart and was based on your feelings about her or him as a person. Then point out her or his special qualities as an individual, especially those that are unique to her or him, and how much you love these qualities.

■ *Don't deny the fact that being an adopted child is different from being a biological one.*

You should certainly communicate to your adopted child that you love her or him just as much as if she or he were your biological child—and if there are biological children in the family, just as much as you love them. However, avoid belittling your child's feelings that her or his situation is different from that of a biological child.

For example, adopted children often worry about whether their biological heritage is compatible with, or as fortunate as, the heritage of their adoptive parents. They also often worry about their biological parents showing up unexpectedly and taking them away from their adoptive mother and father. These worries should be addressed and alleviated, but they shouldn't be treated as if they were foolish or unwarranted.

Invite your adopted child to discuss any feelings of difference in more detail. Help her or him deal with them but don't imply that there is anything "wrong" with having them. Remember that your child is the first and foremost authority on how she or he feels. And unless you yourself were adopted, your child knows a great deal more about how it feels.

Your adopted child needs to know that you can accept and appreciate her or his sense of things even though you aren't biologically related. Contradicting your child's genuine impressions of difference will only create even more feelings of alienation.

■*Don't expect your child to resolve all troublesome feelings about being adopted.*

People who are adopted often describe the knowledge that they are adopted as a wound that never completely heals. Be prepared for your school-age adopted child to exhibit occasional age-appropriate symptoms of this wound, such as the following:

■ accusations that you are not her or his "real" parent (including, possibly, allegations that she or he has been kidnapped by you);

■ exceptional problems getting along with siblings, especially if they are your biological children;

■ fantasies about being reunited with, or rescued by, her or his biological parents;

■ refusal to cooperate in family activities;

■ unusual shyness around relatives;

■ overly—or inappropriately—intense emotional reaction to television shows, movies, stories, or pictures featuring parent-and-child relationships.

■*Prepare family and friends to deal with your child's adoption-related concerns in a comfortable and constructive manner.*

Let them know everything that your child knows about the adoption.

Also, let them know how you'd like them to respond if your child expresses to them any concerns about being adopted.

Another adult, especially a close friend who is not a blood relative of a parent, can be an especially helpful confidant and role model for an adopted child. Like the child, this person is not biologically linked to the family but is nevertheless an integral part of it.

Encourage all such relationships between your adopted child and appropriate adults in your circle of close family members and friends. One or more of these "special" relationships could prove invaluable in giving your insecure child a stronger sense of connection to the world around her or him.

■ *Consider seeking professional help if your child's adoption-related concerns are seriously interfering with her or his well-being or that of the family.*

If your child exhibits frequent symptoms of distress about her or his adopted status for longer than a month, it could be a sign of deeply rooted emotional problems, some of which may not even be directly related to the adoption. If you believe this may be the case, don't hesitate to seek professional help.

Professional help for the family may be advisable if you feel that you and/or other members of your family are suffering unduly as a result of your child's adoption-related concerns. Evidence of such suffering would include a month or more of any of the following situations:

■ frequent episodes of intense sibling rivalry;

■ profound and unshakable parental anxiety about the adopted child's emotional state;

■ consistent disruption of family gatherings due to the actions—or withdrawal—of the adopted child.

11.

School

When school enters a child's universe, it has an overwhelming impact. The educational experience in itself accounts for only a part of that impact. At least equally significant is that the child begins to lead an emotionally demanding double life upon attending school.

At home, the school-age child is a clearly dependent, beloved, and secure family member; but at school the situation is different. There the child is a relatively independent class member who must work to earn approval from peers and teachers in order to feel accepted and secure.

Most of the time children are able to make the transition from one life to the other remarkably well. The emotional support, self-esteem, and intimate knowledge of human behavior that they derive from family life help them achieve their personal objectives in school life both academically and socially.

However, when a child's home life and school life are not in harmony with each other, the side effects can be devastating emotionally. Problems at school can easily create trouble at home, and vice versa. The child forced to go back and forth from one troubled life to another is doubly vulnerable to anxiety, depression, frustration, anger, fear, and despair.

For example, a child upset by tension among family members may be distracted from her or his lessons in school. This could result in poor academic performance, which might exacerbate tensions between the child and her or his parents. Or the same child might start taking out her or his frustrations with family members on her or his teachers and peers, thus causing behavior problems at school that the parents must ultimately address.

Another example of trouble transferring from one life to another is the possible dilemma of a child who experiences problems at school—either academically or socially—while at the same time enjoying a comparatively happy home life. The child may go through a long period of concealing any school-related problems from her or his parents, thus creating a rift between parent and child that can't help but widen as long as the deception continues. Or the child may react to school-related problems by being rebellious, withdrawn, or generally out of sorts at home—a reaction she or he can't afford to display at school.

As the parent of a school-age child, you need to make every effort to ensure that your child's home life and school life are in productive harmony with each other. Here are suggestions to help you meet that goal:

■ *Encourage your child to talk about school life at home.*

Don't just confine your expression of interest to a routine, open-ended greeting like "How was your day at school?" Occasionally each week, at quiet times when there is little risk of distraction, initiate a more in depth conversation about school.

Keep track of specific names, events, and details your child has told you so that you can refer to them as a means of initiating such conversations. Also, be sure to inquire about your child's classmates, social activities, and teacher(s) as well as about academic subjects.

■ *Consult your child's teacher regularly and frequently about academic, behavioral, and social matters.*

Whenever you feel that you don't know what's happening in your child's school life or that she or he is having school-related problems or that her or his life at school might shed some light on problems at home, don't hesitate to set up a parent-teacher conference. In fact, it's a good idea to consult with your child's teacher at least every couple of months, even if there are no specific issues prompting such a consultation.

During any consultation—whether it's for a specific reason or simply for a general "checkup"—always express to the teacher that you are willing to do anything that will help benefit your child's school life. If serious disagreements develop between you and the teacher, make every effort to resolve them peacefully, even if it means conferring jointly with the school principal. Otherwise, you may be inadvertently putting your child in an extremely awkward position—torn between loyalty to you and allegiance to a teacher.

■ *Keep informed about your child's curriculum, school, and school system.*

You want to make sure not only that you know what's going on in your child's school life but also that you have a sound basis for evaluating whether or not your child is receiving a high-quality education in a supportive environment. Attend all school-sponsored meetings and those conducted by parent-teacher organizations. Also, routinely read about your school and school system in local periodicals.

In these meetings and readings as well as in conferences with your child's teacher, seek specific information about what your child is learning and how it is being taught. Other issues to explore are teacher qualifications, classroom and school disciplinary policies, and counseling services and educational options that are available to your child.

■ *Help your child do homework without actually doing it yourself.*

Set up with your child a specific time when homework should be done (such as one hour after dinner) and enforce the routine. It will help develop good study habits. Show an interest in the schoolwork that your child is assigned to do at home and make sure that she or he has space and materials to do the work to the best of her or his ability. However, if your child comes to you with specific questions about the work, help her or him discover the answers independently instead of simply supplying the answers.

■ *Avoid tying grades for academic performance to a strong punishment-and-reward system.*

Your child should learn to regard success in academic performance as its own reward and failure as its own punishment. It's good to express pleasure when a child does particularly well in school and occasionally to celebrate. It's also appropriate to express caring concern when a child does particularly poorly in school and, if circumstances warrant it, to insist that more attention to schoolwork take precedence over other activities. However, try as much as possible not to set up a rigid routine of rewards and punishments: for example, a half hour more TV watching a night for good grades or a half hour less for bad ones. The routine in itself can easily become a source of emotional conflict.

■ *Help motivate your child to be interested in what is being taught in school.*

Begin with what already interests your child and draw connections between it and school subjects. You might, for example, try turning your child's love of movies into an enthusiasm for reading by giving her or him a book related to a favorite movie; or you might try turning your child's fondness for games into a love for research challenges in general.

In addition, look for subtle opportunities to apply school knowledge to practical activities at home. For example, involve your child in applying mathematical skills to cooking from recipes or buying paint for covering a certain area of space.

∎ *Make a special effort to maintain a stable, supportive home environment during major turning points in your child's school life.*
Occasions like the first few months of school life, the beginning and end of each school year, and the transition from elementary school to middle school or junior high are particularly stressful times for children. Try as much as possible to avoid major changes or problems at home during these periods. The resulting calm in your child's home life will help her or him handle more effectively the turbulence in her or his school life.

Repeating and Skipping Grades

What can parents and teachers do when a child just doesn't seem to be compatible with other children in her or his chronologically assigned grade level? One possibility is to assign the child to a grade level that is likely to be more appropriate, even though virtually all the children in that grade level are a different age.

If the child is socially and/or intellectually more advanced than her or his age peers, it may be helpful to skip a grade (technically known as a "double promotion"). If the child is socially or intellectually less advanced, it may be helpful to repeat a grade.

However, changing a child's grade level is not always beneficial in such situations. It may even make matters worse. A relatively slow child may suffer even more loss of self-esteem and motivation if forced to be "one year behind" chronological peers for the rest of school life. Inevitably, much of the repeated year will be made up of material the child has already learned, which may only increase the child's boredom and dissatisfaction with school.

A good student who skips a grade may feel physically, socially, and emotionally "one year behind" classmates at the new grade level for the rest of the school year, which could significantly reduce the student's former initiative and pride. Inevitably, she or he will miss important academic material in that "lost" year.

On the other hand, a poorly performing student who gets an extra year to catch up—academically, socially, and emotionally—may turn into a competent or even an outstanding student and remain so for the rest of her or his school life. A student who skips a year may have been rescued from stagnating at a grade level that would have offered insufficient intellectual challenges.

Before allowing your child to step out of sequence from her or his "regular" grade level, consider the following important issues.

REPEATING A GRADE

■ Is your child experiencing difficulties in *every* academic subject or just in some of them? If your child is doing fine in just one area, there's reason to hope that she or he is capable of improving in the other areas with special assistance, thus reducing the argument for holding her or him back a grade.

■ In addition to poor academic performance, is your child less mature socially or emotionally than most other children in her or his present grade level? If not, then the case for holding her or him back a grade is much weaker.

■ Has your child's teacher carefully analyzed her or his educational needs and offered an informed opinion about why she or he has academic problems—and, possibly, social and emotional problems as well? Don't agree to let your child repeat a grade unless such an analysis has been made to your satisfaction.

■ Does your child know all the reasons why she or he may have to repeat a grade? Have you allowed your child to express her or his feelings about the possibility of repeating a grade? Have you and your child's teachers informed her or him about all the potential problems and opportunities associated with such a step? If the answer to any of these questions is no, don't allow any action to be taken. Should your child be—or become— adamantly opposed to repeating a grade, the chances are almost nil that the strategy will be helpful.

■ Can you fully support the decision to have your child repeat a grade, and are you prepared to give your child the extra attention and assistance that may be required to adjust to such a transition? If not, then rethink the situation.

SKIPPING A GRADE

■ Is your child more advanced in *all* academic areas relative to other children in her or his chronologically assigned grade level? And is she or he so advanced in these areas that she or he can be a top achiever in the new grade level? If the answer to either of these questions is no, then skipping a grade may create academic problems as well as, or instead of, academic progress. Explore other options for intellectual challenge.

■ In addition to being academically more advanced than other children her or his age, is your child more mature socially and emotionally? If not, then it's highly questionable that she or he will adjust well to the higher grade level.

■ Is your child physically smaller or less developed than most other children her or his age level? If so, then your child is likely to feel grotesquely out of place among children in a higher grade level. Such a feeling can have a very damaging effect on your child academically, socially, and emotionally.

■ Does your child know all the reasons why she or he is considered eligible to skip a grade? Has your child been given every chance to express her or his feelings about the idea? And has your child been fully informed about the possible problems and opportunities involved in such a move? Don't take any action unless the answer to all these questions is yes.

■ Do you firmly believe that your child's skipping a grade is the best action to take given her or his situation, and are you prepared to offer your child the extra attention and assistance that such a move may require? If the answer to either of these questions is no, pursue some other alternative.

12.

Friendship

Friendships during the school-age years can be a great source of emotional strength not only at the time but also later in life. Through such early experiments in intimacy, children develop self-awareness, self-confidence, and self-esteem. In addition, they learn to rely on human relationships as vehicles for reaching beyond the self to enlarge and enrich one's frame of reference. Thus, friendships help carry them through emotional crises and conflicts in their ongoing lives that might otherwise cause lingering psychological problems.

By contrast, children who remain friendless during their school years are more likely to develop negative, compensatory behaviors that actually trigger emotional crises and conflicts. Specifically, children suffering from loneliness during their middle years are more susceptible—then or later—to academic failure, eating disorders, substance abuse, sex-related troubles, and even suicidal thoughts than their more sociable peers are.

Typically, school-age children between the ages of six and nine form relatively casual friendships with a number of children. Many of these friendships subsist on the basis of a single activity. For example, a seven-year-old girl may have one friend for ice-skating, another for riding bikes, and a third with whom to eat lunch at school. There may be several "multiactivity" friends (neighborhood kids tend to fall into this category) with whom a child in this age range spends a great deal of time; but, generally, personal allegiances to these friends are fairly simple and nondemanding. It's not unusual for friendships of any type to come and go in a matter of a few months.

Around the time a child reaches age nine, friendship becomes a far more serious enterprise. By then a child has been socializing enough with her or his peers to appreciate the value of having close, dependable allies. Even more significant, a child this old is emotionally mature enough to empathize with peers and is therefore more interested in sharing thoughts and feelings with particularly compatible friends than a younger child is.

As a result, a school-age child over nine years old usually seeks, or possesses, an intense and demanding relationship with one special friend of the same sex, the so-called best friend. This relationship may remain a vital source of pleasure and pain for years, since the child feeds it, is fed by it, and frets about it. In general, all friendships will tend to be more complex and more long-lasting than earlier ones were.

The specific reasons why a school-age child makes, or doesn't make, friends vary from child to child and include a wide range of purely situational factors, such as the nature of the child's home life and personal interests. However, children who have ongoing difficulty making friends tend to fall into one of two categories: those who are too shy or those who are overly aggressive. It's dangerous to make too many assumptions based on such tendencies, for shyness and aggression in themselves may not be problems at all. They may even be assets in making friends. It's the extremes of those traits that cause problems. An excessively aggressive child can easily turn into a bully; a very shy one can easily turn into a bully's target.

Whether they are overly shy, overly aggressive, or just plain friendless, not all isolated children suffer from loneliness, nor do all children suffering from it go on to experience emotionally troubled lives. In some cases, isolated or lonely children evolve into exceptionally resourceful and creative people, perhaps because their solitary state challenged them to excel.

Nevertheless, as a parent, you should do what you reasonably can to foster your child's social skills and opportunities, providing her or him every chance to enjoy the undeniable benefits of healthy peer friendships. You should also be prepared to deal effectively with the emotional pain that friends—or a lack of them—can cause your child.

Here are some guidelines:

■ Be especially cautious about intervening in your child's social life.

As much as possible, grant your child the emotional growth experience of finding her or his own ways of making friends and of dealing with rejection. Friendship is one area of life in which a child wants, needs, and should receive a certain amount of independence and privacy.

Also, don't jump to conclusions about your child's social life—or apparent lack of it. This includes making hasty judgments that your child is not getting along with friends, is suffering from not having them, or is involved in "undesirable" friendships.

Before acting on any serious concerns you may have, check your impressions against those of other adults who are knowledgeable about your child, including her or his teacher. Your vision of the situation may easily be very selective, biased, or misinformed.

You might also ask your child's siblings discreet and casual questions about your child's friendships, if you think it would help. Just be very careful not to put your child in an awkward or embarrassing situation by doing so.

■ *Encourage your child to talk about her or his friendships.*
Your best source of information about your child's friendships, and the first one you should consult, is your child her- or himself. Make it easy for your child to talk about friends—or about life without them. You can do this by expressing your interest regularly and casually, withholding your personal judgments, recalling specific names and events that your child has mentioned previously, and sharing appropriate memories of your own past and present friendships.

These conversations can be just as helpful to your child as they are to you. They provide a forum for expressing and thereby realizing true feelings about particular friendships or about not having the kinds of friendships she or he may want.

■ *Help your child understand social cues and behaviors.*
Children often have difficulty relating well to their peers because they don't know how to read the verbal and nonverbal signals that people commonly use to indicate their feelings. For example, some children don't realize that a playmate's mild teasing may be a sign of interest and even affection rather than dislike. And some children unintentionally alienate a favorably disposed playmate by continuing to seek the playmate's company after she or he has indirectly expressed a desire to be alone for a while.

Take advantage of every opportunity to educate your child in a casual manner regarding the social meaning of particular behaviors. One way of doing this is to offer nonthreatening commentary on peer-related incidents your child tells you about or to make instructive side remarks about interpersonal scenes that both you and your child witness either in real life or on television.

■ *Teach your child basic rules regarding how to handle social situations successfully.*
Your child should be told—and made to understand—that grabbing, whining, tattling, bullying, lying, and stealing are *not* socially rewarding behaviors. And your child should also know what behaviors *are* socially rewarding: sharing, cooperating, being trustworthy and dependable, respecting other people's bodies and property, showing concern for other people's problems, and helping other people enjoy themselves.

In addition, take appropriate opportunities to talk with your child about the basic elements of conflict resolution: stating what one wants, listening to what the other one wants, negotiating peacefully, and working out a compromise. Role-playing with your child is one of the best ways to communicate these basic elements, so be alert for specific, real-life situations to role-play that come to your attention (e.g., disagreements or fights that your child tells you about).

■ *Help your child become involved in peer-group activities.*
Try interesting your child in joining a sports team, a scouting group, a hobby club, or a community action group. Also, take your child to places and events where there will be other children with whom to socialize, such as a park, a beach, a fair, a neighborhood gathering, a group picnic, an amusement park, an environmental center, a children's theater production, or a holiday-related public event.

■ *Make sure that your child receives loving one-on-one attention at home.*
The depressing or anxiety-producing effects of having trouble with friends or of having no friends at all can be greatly alleviated if a child feels that she or he has warm, supportive, and entertaining relationships with other family members. Over time, such relationships can also help a socially awkward child develop the confidence and skills needed to form more satisfying friendships with peers.

How to Tell:
Excessively Shy?
Overly Aggressive?

Signs that a child may be extremely *shy* include any combination of the following symptoms lasting longer than two months:

■ repeated refusal to participate in peer activities;

■ consistent lack of reference, or disparaging reference, to peers in conversations;

■ repeated incidents of being victimized by other children (taken advantage of, taunted, hit);

■ apparent preference for being left alone;

■ recurring episodes of excessive clinging to parents;

■ persistent fearfulness or depression.

Signs that a child may be excessively *aggressive* include any combination of the following symptoms lasting longer than two months:

■ repeated incidents of victimizing other children (taking advantage of, taunting, hitting);

■ consistent inability to be alone;

■ repeated episodes of angry screaming or tantrums;

■ persistent defiance of parents and other authority figures;

■ numerous acts of physical destruction or stealing.

The Bully and the Bullied

Teasing and being teased is an inalienable part of any school-age friendship. So is fighting, which means sometimes losing and sometimes winning. However, a bully and her or his victim are locked into a relationship that is primarily, if not entirely, characterized by teasing or fighting, with one kid always dominating the other.

Sometimes the two individuals involved in the bully-victim relationship mistakenly think of it as a friendship—and so might their peers, their teachers, and their parents. At other times, the two individuals—and everyone else who observes them closely—have no illusions that the relationship is anything more than a vicious and decidedly unfriendly game.

Curiously enough, school-age bullies and their victims tend to gravitate toward each other. Bullies tend to be aggressive people by nature who subconsciously seek someone on whom they can vent their general anger, fear, and frustration. Victims, on the other hand, tend to be shy people by nature who subconsciously seek someone to punish them for being (in their own opinion) generally weak, inferior, or incompetent. Thus, while a bully-victim relationship may *appear* to be one-sided, with the bully always being responsible, in fact it usually takes two kids to make a bully and two to make a victim.

If you suspect that your child is bullying, or is being bullied by, another child, here are some ways to help break up the bully-victim relationship:

BULLY

■ *Educate your child about the rights of other children.*
Don't just assume that your child already knows the difference
between right and wrong in matters of social conduct. Help
her or him empathize with peers, especially those to whom she
or he seems especially insensitive. In conversations with your
child about these people, encourage her or him to imagine how
they must feel, what they must want, and what they deserve.

■ *Set clear and firm rules regarding the social behavior
you expect.*
Tell her or him that any abusive behavior toward another
child—such as picking a fight, teasing beyond the limits of
fairness, threatening serious harm, or damaging personal
property—is not allowed. Also, establish punishments for such
behavior (such as "grounding") and stick to them.

One of the most effective punishments for a child who bullies
others is to impose isolation in a quiet environment. Usually,
this kind of child dislikes being alone and still, which accounts
to some degree for her or his aggressive interactions with others. Being forced to spend time alone and still not only punishes
the child but also works in the long run to make the child
more capable of self-control.

■ *Make a special effort to teach your child acceptable
behaviors for getting what she or he wants.*
This involves teaching your child, as palatably as you can, the
benefits and techniques of negotiating with other people instead of strong-arming them. Take advantage of spontaneous
incidents in day-to-day life to make important points. Also,
try role-playing situations that your child has encountered or
is about to confront, letting your child take turns playing both
roles. Role-playing is particularly effective with school-age
girls, whose bullying tends to be more verbal than that of boys.

■ *Involve your child in "safe" activities where she or he
can have fun with others in a polite and constructive
manner.*
The more practice your child has in getting along with others
without resorting to bullying, the better equipped she or he
will be to avoid it whenever the impulse strikes. The trick is
to steer your child toward situations in which interaction with
others will be directly, or indirectly, moderated.

Encourage your child's participation in family gatherings and supervised outings and sports activities (which are often effective in channeling an aggressive child's excess energy). The presence of adults during such activities will help discourage the would-be bully; as a result, she or he will learn to derive more pleasure from being cooperative.

■ *Keep track of your child's bullying offenses and note any patterns.*

You may discover, for example, that your child is most likely to bully other children whenever there's a stressful situation in the family or when experiencing a personal crisis, such as a failure at school or the beginning of a new enterprise. This kind of information can help you prevent, alleviate, or respond to episodes of bullying more successfully.

■ *Set a good example.*

Make sure that you aren't indirectly teaching your child to bully by doing it yourself. And, when appropriate, let your child see you gracefully allowing others to have their way.

■ *Be sure to praise your child's good behavior.*

Frequently, children resort to bullying when they are not getting any attention. If you consistently make a special effort to commend your child for behaving in a polite, cooperative, or compassionate manner, she or he won't need to seek attention through bullying.

VICTIM

■ *Explain to your child that the bully is a troubled person.*

Often the victim of a bully is unable to comprehend why the bully behaves the way she or he does. Sometimes the victim can only conclude that she or he deserves to be bullied and that the bully is in some way a superior person. Tell your child that a bully is an unhappy child and that this unhappiness makes her or him want to hurt other people, which is not fair.

■ *Teach your child "the best way" to cope with a bully.*

You don't want your child to respond to a bully in kind, thereby only escalating the potential danger of the situation, nor do you want your child to have to cower in terror every time she or he is bullied. The proper strategy lies in the middle ground: While refusing to let the bully bother you, look the bully straight in the eye, tell her or him to stop, and then walk away from the situation in a firm and dignified manner. Even though this strategy may not always work, you should let your child know that it is the "best way" to try to get the bully to stop.

Practice role-playing variations of this basic strategy with your child, taking turns playing each role. In relationships where assuming the middle ground seems especially difficult or risky, advise your child to stay away from the bully whenever it's convenient to do so.

■ *Encourage your child to talk about her or his relationships, especially those with bullies.*

These conversations will help both you and your child put the bullying into perspective. Be sure to tell your child that if the bully ever resorts to physical violence, then she or he should immediately report the incident to a responsible adult (teacher or parent).

■ *Engage your child in activities, especially interpersonal ones, that will help build self-esteem.*

The victim of a bully needs to bolster her or his self-confidence. Encourage participation in fun activities that make her or him feel safe and competent but also involve a certain amount of self-assertion: games, sports, hobbies, contests, and/or community services.

■ *Praise your child for any acts of skill mastery, personal achievement, courage, or leadership.*

This kind of feedback helps alleviate the fear and self-contempt that a bully can inspire. Just make sure that your praise is sincere and not extravagant.

When a child is praised for such acts in the presence of a bully (or, for that matter, when a bully is praised for good behavior in the presence of her or his victim), much of the interpersonal chemistry that creates a bully-victim relationship may be neutralized. No longer do the roles seem so clear-cut.

Interpersonal Versus Intrapersonal Intelligence

Child psychologists and psychiatrists often speak of a child's "*inter*personal" as opposed to "*intra*personal" intelligence. Interpersonal intelligence refers to a child's knowledge and skills involving social relationships. By contrast, intrapersonal intelligence refers to a child's knowledge and skills involving her or his own inner self, independent of the outside world.

A child with a high degree of interpersonal intelligence is one who understands the dynamics of making and keeping friends, who can figure out how to lead others, and who is adept at cooperating, compromising, and resolving conflicts within a group context. Interpersonal intelligence tends to be acquired by extensive socialization in a variety of contexts, such as assuming an active role in a large family, engaging in different types of play and competition with various friends, and performing tasks in concert with other individuals and work teams.

A child with a high degree of intrapersonal intelligence is one who is adept at cultivating self-knowledge as well as knowledge for the sake of personal development, who is capable of self-entertaiment (i.e., enjoying solitude) for extended periods of time, and who can identify and formulate her or his personal needs, motivations, and feelings apart from those of others.

Every child has some degree of both types of intelligence, but most children become more intelligent in one of these two ways than in the other. Typically, a child who is extroverted by nature will wind up having a better-developed interpersonal intelligence; one who is introverted by nature will wind up having a better-developed intrapersonal intelligence.

As a result, extroverted children often suffer psychological problems because of a deficiency in intrapersonal intelligence (i.e., a lack of knowing their "inner selves"). Introverted children generally have the opposite problem: They suffer psychological problems because of a deficiency in interpersonal intelligence (i.e., a lack of knowing how to interact effectively with others).

When such imbalances are first detected by parents or educators, they are often treated inappropriately. Simply pressuring an apparent bookworm into joining a soccer team so that she or he will become more interpersonally intelligent could easily backfire. The bookworm may experience so much unpleasantness and even trauma playing soccer that she or he will retreat even further into books. The same kind of thing might happen if a soccer lover is forced to read the complete works of Shakespeare to become more intrapersonally intelligent. The soccer-lover's dislike of reading may instead be reinforced.

Much can be done to correct a troubled child's imbalance in interpersonal versus intrapersonal intelligence, but it must be done carefully, with full respect for the child's personal capabilities and vulnerabilities. Fortunately, most psychologists and psychiatrists are well qualified to assist individual children (along with their parents, teachers, and caretakers) in identifying the particular training methods and experiences that will most help them develop the type of intelligence they lack.

13.
Television

Aside from school and family, no human institution has a greater impact than television on the life of a child during the middle years. Experts estimate that American children between the ages of six and thirteen spend an average of three and a half hours a day watching TV. Not only does TV give them a considerable amount of their day-to-day entertainment and information, it also plays a major role in shaping their attitudes, behaviors, and value systems.

It is this latter fact that worries many parents and educators. Their principal questions:

■ How emotionally healthy can it be for children to spend so much of their time watching TV, since it's such a passive activity and such a large proportion of TV fare is violent?

■ Does watching TV stifle a child's imagination and creativity by keeping her or him from engaging in more constructive leisure-time activities, like reading, conversing, playing games, and simply daydreaming? Or does it actually stimulate a child's imagination and creativity in ways that these other activities cannot?

■ Does watching violence on TV inspire a child to be cruel in real life? Or does it provide a vicarious means for the child to discharge the negative emotions that she or he already harbors so that she or he is less likely to be violent in real life?

For the most part, clear answers to these questions are elusive. While watching television is undeniably a passive activity, which can, indeed, result in physical and emotional lethargy, it can also be a very calming activity, encouraging otherwise restless and unruly children to relax and pay attention. And while watching television certainly does detract from the time kids spend engaging in other activities that are mentally and emotionally enriching, it is not necessarily time lost. In addition to broadening their knowledge by watching newscasts, documentaries, and informational programming, kids can exercise their minds and emotions by becoming involved in television dramas, comedies, and movies.

Nevertheless, child psychiatrists and psychologists who have studied the effects of TV violence on children are becoming more and more convinced that they are mainly negative. Specifically, they are concerned about the following tendencies:

■ Children are likely to mimic the violence they see on television, either playfully or seriously.

■ Children are inclined to identify with particular victims or victimizers and to carry these identifications into real-life situations.

■ Children can become desensitized to the horror of brutality after witnessing so many violent images.

■ Children can reach the point where they regard violence as an acceptable mode of behavior, perhaps even a way to solve their problems.

By following the suggestions listed below, you can help control the amount of TV violence to which your child is exposed as well as help prevent TV viewing in general from absorbing too much of your child's time and energy:

■ *Don't permit your child to watch TV programs that are offensive.*
As much as practical, help your child plan in advance which programs will be watched, making sure to avoid programs that you think might be too violent, sexually suggestive, or stressful. If you aren't involved in the advance planning, then ask your child what programs she or he is going to watch that day and screen—either in advance or while it's being watched—any program that concerns you.

If you discover your child watching a television program that you think is too violent, sexually suggestive, or stressful, express your concern and ask your child to choose another program or another activity besides watching TV. Be firm and don't hesitate to change the channel or turn off the TV yourself if your child refuses to do so.

■ *Help your child distinguish between events on TV and those in real life.*
When you and your child witness an offensive act of violence on TV, be sure to draw attention to the fact that the "act" is staged and involves actors and props. Clarify anything that isn't realistic about the situation. For example, victims of television violence typically appear to recover more often—and much faster—than victims of real-life violence.

Also, when appropriate, take care to distinguish between nonviolent situations depicted on TV and their real-life counterparts. For example, if your children cite a sitcom parent as being funnier and wiser than you are, point out that sitcom parents don't really live with their TV children, that they have a team of writers giving them lines, and that they get to rehearse the same situation numerous times until they get it right.

■ *Set limits and conditions regarding the hours per day your child can watch TV.*

Given the total amount of time in a typical school-age child's day, three and a half hours of watching television is excessive, leaving very little time for homework, chores, reading, solitary play, or interaction with others. One hour—or, on special occasions, two hours—is a much more appropriate time limit; and *no* TV viewing should be permitted if it means that there won't be time to do chores or homework.

Whatever time limit you set, be specific about it and include time your child spends watching television with other family members as part of her or his personal time allotment. You may also want to set a time span within which TV viewing must fall (e.g., between 7:00 and 9:00 P.M.). Any special extensions should be negotiated in advance and involve a particular program that has special merit.

The clearer and more firmly enforced your TV rules are, the better they will work. Because watching TV is such a passive activity, it's very easy for an hour to drift into two or three. And rules governing TV can become ineffective if you permit too much leeway or bargaining. For these reasons, it's important to be very sparing about using extra hours of TV watching as a reward.

On the other hand, remember that your goal is *not* necessarily to allow as little TV watching as possible. It can be very beneficial to your child, providing not only entertainment and information but also a field of reference to be shared with peers. Instead of discrediting TV altogether, your goal is to keep certain programs from having a negative impact on your child's life and to prevent TV watching in general from overwhelming her or his leisure time.

■ *Suggest and/or arrange activities for your child to replace television watching.*

Just cutting off your child's TV-viewing hours without proposing alternative activities can be counterproductive. If there is nothing else to do, the child may miss TV so much that she or he will come to value it even more.

In addition to suggesting that your child play with a toy, pursue a hobby, or do something else alone that is pleasurable, try proposing fun activities that you can engage in together. For example, you might play games, bake cookies, or go for a walk.

■ *From time to time, experiment with a "no TV" night.*

When it seems appropriate—that is, when there's nothing on TV that's especially interesting and you can propose an alternative activity— try declaring a "no TV" night. Make sure you refer to this night deliberately as a "no TV" night so that your child feels a sense of achievement in simply not watching TV. A particularly appropriate time is after you've had one or more nights of extended TV watching.

■ *Reform your own bad TV habits.*

Set a good example of TV viewing by adopting these policies yourself:

> ■ Never leave the TV set on without watching it.

> ■ Avoid watching violent programming, at least while your child is at home.

> ■ Avoid doing other things in front of the TV set, thus implying that TV makes a good "background" activity.

> ■ Try cutting down on the number of hours per day that you watch TV.

> ■ Do other things with your visitors besides always watching TV.

> ■ Let your children see you choosing specific programs in advance rather than simply channel hopping to find the best program on the air.

14.
Psychotherapy

The middle years of a child's life are normally characterized by all sorts of trial-and-error experiences in living and therefore all sorts of transitory crises, problems, fears, misbehaviors, and mistakes. Thus, whenever a school-age child appears to be experiencing emotional stress, it can be very difficult for parents to determine objectively whether psychotherapeutic help is necessary.

Perhaps the best way for you, as a parent, to approach any such determination in the case of your child is to make a separate evaluation of each of the four main areas of your child's world: home, school, social life, and personal life. If there seem to have been serious problems lasting for several months in more than one area, then a professional evaluation of your child's overall emotional state may be advisable.

Among the issues to consider in each separate area of your child's world are the following:

HOME

■ Do you and your child frequently quarrel? Why? How intense are these quarrels? How well does your child recover from them? Do you repeatedly quarrel over the same issue without making much progress? Why?

■ Does your child frequently quarrel with his or her siblings? Why? How intense are the quarrels? How well does your child recover from them? What effect do they have on her or his siblings? Why? Do they repeatedly quarrel over the same issue without making much progress? Why?

■ Is your child consistently unhappy and withdrawn at home? Why? Does this behavior interfere with family life? How?

■ Does your child consistently avoid one or more members of the family in particular? Why? How does this avoidance affect the person or persons who are avoided?

■ Has your child's behavior at home undergone any significant and lasting change for the worse recently? How so? Why?

SCHOOL

■ Is your child's academic performance consistently poor? How so? Why?

■ Does your child repeatedly exhibit behavior problems at school? How so? Why?

■ Does your child frequently express unhappiness about school? How so? Why?

■ Has your child's behavior at school recently undergone any significant and lasting change for the worse? How so? Why?

SOCIAL LIFE

■ Does your child frequently quarrel with peers? Why? How intense are the quarrels? How well does your child recover from them? What effect do they have on peers? Are the quarrels repeatedly over the same issue without any progress being made? Why?

■ Does your child consistently avoid peer contact? Why? Are there particular peers that she or he avoids? Why?

■ Does your child frequently express fear, dissatisfaction, and anger regarding peer relationships? How so? Why?

■ Does your child appear to suffer from a lack of friends? How so? Why does she or he lack friends?

PERSONAL LIFE

■ Does your child frequently express boredom or an inability to find things to do? How well does she or he handle such situations?

■ Does your child appear to suffer from a lack of self-esteem? How so? Why?

■ Does your child engage in any self-punishing behavior or in solitary activities that appear to you to be unhealthy or unsavory? How so? Why?

■ Does your child appear to suffer from a lack of interests or initiative? How so? Why?

If you have reason to believe that your child's emotional health should be evaluated by a professional, don't hesitate to take action. The sooner you arrange for the evaluation, the better the chances are that you can catch any problems before they become even more serious. The evaluation itself may or may not reveal the need for actual psychotherapy.

As a rule, psychotherapeutic interventions involving school-age children are relatively brief and pragmatic. Individual sessions typically last from forty-five minutes to two hours. In some cases, one or two sessions may be sufficient. For example, a concerned parent may simply need professional reassurance that her or his child's psychological development is progressing normally or professional advice on strategies and activities that will foster more satisfying parent-child relations. In other cases, effective intervention may require weekly or biweekly sessions for several months. Specific goals for psychotherapy of school-age children generally include helping parents interpret their child's emotional state more accurately, increasing the quality and quantity of a child's—and a family's—social supports, and assisting family members in coping more productively with stressors outside the family.

Case-by-case diagnostic techniques and treatments involving children between the ages of six and thirteen vary considerably according to the specific situation. Generally speaking, parental interviews are always a major part of the process. Parents are asked about their perceptions of their child and about their relationship with her or him and with other family members, including their own parents.

In addition to parental interviews, doctors and therapists rely on "play therapy" and direct interviews with the child. In play therapy, a child acts out or discusses her or his emotions and concerns in the context of playing with toys and games provided by the doctor or therapist.

Play therapy's indirect approach to eliciting a child's feelings and experiences avoids some of the problems that can arise in directly interviewing someone this young. Potential problems of this nature include: the chance that the questions themselves might "lead" the responses; the risk that the child might be frightened by the dialogue; and the possibility that the child's replies might be inaccurate because of comprehension or communication difficulties or the child's wish to conceal the truth due to fear, guilt, or a desire to please.

Here are some issues to consider in finding the right doctor or therapist, and the right type of therapy, for you, your child, and your family:

1. Before you begin your search, establish what you consider to

be the problem that you want addressed and the goal that you want achieved.

First, write down your answers to the following five questions, bearing in mind that some of your answers may overlap:

a. What specific behaviors have I observed indicating that my child may be experiencing emotional turmoil? (To whatever extent possible, give dates, times of day, settings, and circumstantial surroundings.)

b. How would I define this emotional turmoil? (In other words, if you had to make a diagnosis, what would it be?)

c. What might be the cause(s) of this turmoil? (Include any speculations and conclusive opinions you may have, being careful to distinguish between the two categories.)

d. In what different ways has this emotional turmoil been bothersome or detrimental to my child, to me, and to other members of the family? (Be as specific as possible, as you were directed to be in answering question a.)

e. How have I tried to better the situation? (Indicate which methods have been at least partially successful and which have failed altogether.)

Once you have answered all five questions to the best of your ability, write down a fairly succinct (one- or two-sentence) description of what you think the *problem* is. Next, write an equally succinct description of the *goal* that you want to achieve related to this problem: that is, what you would like to see happen *as a result* of psychotherapeutic intervention.

These statements, as well as the question-and-answer background material, will be enormously helpful to you in interviewing possible doctors or therapists. They will also be enormously helpful to the doctor or therapist you choose in her or his efforts to diagnose and treat your child successfully.

2. Familiarize yourself with the major types of therapy that are available.

The sheer variety of therapy labels is bewildering to the outsider: psychoanalytic (Freudian, Jungian, Adlerian, or otherwise), cognitive, behavioral, existential, Gestalt, transactional, reality-oriented, rational-emotive, and so on. However, for the purpose of interviewing potential doctors or therapists to work with a child between the ages of six and thirteen, all you need is a very basic awareness of three broad categories of psychotherapy: psychodynamic therapy, behavioral therapy, and family-oriented therapy. Let's consider each category individually:

■ *Psychodynamic therapy* is geared toward getting the child to identify, understand, and self-manage her or his emotional problems. It depends heavily on effective verbal communication between the doctor or therapist and the child, so it may not be appropriate for younger children in this age range, who may not be very fluent in verbal communication. It also tends to be relatively long-term compared to other categories of psychotherapy, often involving multiple sessions per week up to a year or two.

■ *Behavioral therapy* is geared toward getting the child to change the way she or he behaves. Instead of focusing squarely on the causes of a particular problem, it concentrates on the symptoms. For example, it might help children learn to control their anger without necessarily getting them to appreciate why they get angry, to be less scared of nightmares regardless of whether they know about their possible source, or to interact more cooperatively with other people even if their feelings about them remain unresolved. It typically takes at least a few months of weekly or biweekly sessions before satisfactory results can be expected.

■ *Family-oriented therapy*, sometimes known as "systems therapy," is one of the types of therapy practiced at Philadelphia Child Guidance Center (PCGC) and the type that PCGC recommends most highly for children of any age. Drawing upon both psychodynamic therapy and behavioral therapy, family-oriented therapy is geared toward generating positive awareness and change in all aspects of the child's world: her or his own mind and behavior as well as the minds and behaviors of those people who directly influence her or his life. In comparison to other therapies, it is much more adaptable to the situation at hand. Satisfactory results may be achieved in just one or two sessions or may take up to a year or two.

Use these very basic distinctions as starting points for discussing with other people (such as knowledgeable advisers and potential doctors or therapists) the particular type or types of psychotherapy that may be appropriate for your unique situation. Also, investigate the literature about child psychotherapy that's available at local libraries and bookstores. The more informed you are about child psychotherapy—whatever form it may take—the more benefit you'll derive from the type you finally choose, whatever it may be.

3. Familiarize yourself with the major types of doctors and therapists that are available.

The three most common practitioners of child-oriented psychotherapy are psychiatrists, psychologists, and social workers. Regardless of the specific title (e.g., "child psychiatrist"), not all of these practitioners have special training or experience in treating children in particular as opposed to people in general. This is an important issue that you will want to investigate with individual practitioners that you interview.

Also, keep in mind that one type of practitioner, all else being equal, is not necessarily more or less desirable than another. Your final determination should be based on how appropriate the individual practitioner is, given the following factors: your child's problem, the goals you've established relating to that problem, the type of therapy you're interested in pursuing, your financial resources, and most important of all, the overall personalities of you and your child.

These warnings having been given, here are brief descriptions of each major type of practitioner.

■ *Psychiatrists* are medical doctors (M.D.s), which means that they have had four years of medical school, one year of internship, and at least two years of residency training in psychiatry. In addition, virtually all child psychiatrists have had two-year fellowships in child psychiatry and are board certified.

One major advantage of a psychiatrist over other types of practitioners is that he or she can diagnose and prescribe treatment for physical problems that may be causing or aggravating a child's emotional problems. A possible disadvantage, depending on your particular situation, is that some psychiatrists (usually not *child* psychiatrists) are inclined to practice only psychodynamic forms of therapy.

■ *Psychologists* have usually earned a doctorate (Ph.D.) in psychology, typically the result of five years of graduate training, including several supervised clinical programs and a year of formal internship. Most states also require postdoctoral experience before licensing. Some states, however, require only a master's degree (M.A.) to become a psychologist.

Although psychologists themselves cannot offer physical diagnosis and prescription, they almost always have close professional relationships with M.D.s whom they can recommend for such services. They are also likely to be more eclectic in their therapeutic style, although there is still a trend among psychologists to favor behavioral therapy.

■ *Social workers* have earned a master's degree in social work (M.S.W.), a process that involves two years of classes and fieldwork.

In addition, some states require two or more years of postgraduate experience before licensing.

While social workers may not have had the extensive academic and clinical training that psychiatrists and psychologists have had, they are, as a rule, much more familiar with—and knowledgeable about— the home, community, and school environments of their clients. This background inclines them to favor family-oriented or systems-oriented therapy over other types of therapy.

Another major issue to consider in choosing a particular type of doctor or therapist is whether the therapy will occur in a *private office* or a *clinic*. Other factors aside, therapy performed in a clinic tends to be more multidimensional: a by-product of the fact that clinics are so often staffed with different types of doctors and therapists, who not only practice different types of therapy but also conduct different kinds of research projects.

---

4. *Make a rough estimate of how much you can afford to spend on your child's therapy*.

It may be impossible to put a price on a child's emotional well-being. However, it's quite possible to determine how much you can afford to spend for psychotherapy without making life much more difficult for yourself and your family—a situation that could only exacerbate your child's emotional problems.

You may have insurance that will cover some or all of the expenses directly incurred as a result of your child's therapy; but in the best of situations there are bound to be some hidden costs. Factor into your budget such possibilities as lost income for days off work, transportation and parking for therapy sessions, and baby-sitting care for other children while you are at the sessions.

In estimating how much you can afford, take into account that private therapy is almost certain to be more expensive than therapy in a clinic. Also, clinics may offer lower fees if you accept therapy from a supervised student therapist or agree to participate in a research project (which typically means being observed, taped, and/or interviewed).

---

5. *Seek several recommendations from a variety of qualified sources*.

Ask relatives and friends who have benefited from the services of child psychiatrists, psychologists, or social workers for their opinions, but also seek leads from more experienced and disinterested parties, such as your pediatrician, family physician, and clergyperson. For the names of certified practitioners in your area, contact the local and national mental-health and professional organizations (see Appendix for a list of suggestions).

6. *Interview different doctors and therapists thoroughly about their credentials, areas of expertise, and therapeutic techniques.*

Among the specific questions you should ask are the following:

■ What is your educational and training background (see issue 3)?

■ Are you board certified? By whom?

■ With what professional organizations are you affiliated (see Appendix for a list)?

■ How long have you practiced in your current capacity?

■ What is your general or preferred style of therapy (see issue 2)?

■ What are your areas of special expertise?

■ How much work have you done with children who are the same age as my child?

■ How much work have you done with the type of problem(s) my child is having (see issue 1)?

■ Would you feel committed to achieving the goal I have in mind (see issue 1)?

■ What kinds of services can I expect from you toward meeting this goal?

■ What kinds of commitment and cooperation would you expect from me and my family in the course of my child's therapy?

■ How, and at what rate, will you keep me informed of the progress my child is making in therapy?

■ How much time do you estimate the therapy might take?

■ How much will it cost, will my insurance or medical assistance help pay the cost, and are there ways to reduce the cost (see issue 4)?

7. *Make sure that you choose a doctor or therapist who respects you and with whom you are comfortable.*

Some doctors or therapists may unintentionally inspire you to feel guilty or incompetent, in which case you should look for someone else. The doctor or therapist you select should be a person who inspires you to feel good about yourself: *re*moralized instead of *de*moralized.

Your answer to each of the following questions should be yes both during your initial interview with a doctor or therapist and throughout the time that the therapy itself is in progress:

■ Does the doctor or therapist take into account *your* theories, opinions, and concerns as well as her or his own?

■ Does the interaction you have with the doctor or therapist seem like a dialogue rather than a monologue on the doctor's or therapist's part?

■ Does the doctor or therapist seem genuinely interested in you and your situation (evidenced by her or his paying close attention to you, maintaining fairly consistent eye contact with you, and regularly soliciting your comments and reactions)?

■ Does the doctor or therapist seem genuinely interested in your child and her or his problems?

■ Does the doctor or therapist make sure that you understand what she or he is doing and saying?

■ Does the doctor or therapist answer all of your questions promptly, thoughtfully, and to the best of her or his ability?

■ Do you leave the doctor's or therapist's company feeling clear about the direction that your child's case will be taking?

■ Do you leave the doctor's or therapist's company feeling generally stronger rather than weaker?

Special Diagnoses: Children in the Middle Years

ATTENTION-DEFICIT HYPERACTIVITY DISORDER

Attention-deficit hyperactivity disorder (ADHD) is the most common psychiatric disorder of childhood, with an overall prevalence rate of 5 percent. It manifests itself most clearly in school as a persistent combination of restlessness, noisiness, an inability to sit still or concentrate, poor socialization, and poor scholastic performance. However, ADHD affects all aspects of a child's life, not just her or his school life, and the victim usually exhibits some signs of ADHD even before school age.

Psychotherapists who suspect ADHD from a child's history will recommend a medical evaluation to determine if there may be some alternative explanation for her or his symptoms: for example, a hearing impairment, hyperthyroidism, a seizure-related condition, and/or an allergy. If ADHD does seem to be the source of the child's problems, then the psychotherapist assists the child and the family in developing coping strategies: for example, procedures that will keep the child focused on individual tasks as they present themselves and help pace the child through the performance of each task in an appropriate manner. When a diagnosis of ADHD is severe and indisputable, tranquilizing medication may also be prescribed.

LEARNING DISABILITIES

A school-age child suffering from a learning disability typically tries hard to follow instructions in school, concentrate on performing well, and complete all assignments in a timely manner. Nevertheless, she or he routinely fails to master assignments and falls far behind other classmates.

Although the precise cause of learning disabilities is not known for sure, it is generally believed that they result from a complication in the nervous system that adversely affects the brain's ability to receive, process, and/or communicate information. Some learning-disabled children also suffer from ADHD, which may be the cause of their particular disability. Overall, learning disabilities affect approximately 15 percent of otherwise capable school-age children.

A psychotherapist who suspects that a child suffers from a learning disability will arrange for appropriate testing with school professionals as well as other specialists. Among the possible treatment procedures for a learning disability are placement in a special class or school, speech or language therapy, and/or parent-driven programs for helping the child cope with the disability, make the most of her or his learning potential, and develop more self-confidence and initiative.

At PCGC: ADHD Evaluation and Treatment

Attention-deficit hyperactivity disorder (ADHD) is one of the most widely researched subjects in child psychology. And yet in many respects it remains a perplexing mystery, with much disagreement among experts about what it is, what causes it, and how it should be treated.

This confusion stems primarily from the fact that each case of ADHD is different. Some sufferers have no other apparent problem than a high degree of distractibility. Others have a whole constellation of problems, including severe personality and learning disorders. As a result, each child with ADHD must be considered apart from all the others, and each evaluation and treatment strategy must be custom-tailored.

The Evaluation and Treatment Program, a joint project of The Children's Hospital of Philadelphia, Children's Seahorse House, and PCGC, serves as an example of how to facilitate effective individual-based evaluation and treatment of ADHD. Children from ages five to fourteen are enrolled by referral.

The therapeutic approach of the program is multimodal. Pediatricians, psychologists, psychiatrists, and social workers form a team that works along with the child and her or his parents to maximize the child's chances for successful management of ADHD. One team member initiates the diagnosis and remains the "case manager," coordinating the various psychological, educational, and medical assessments that are deemed necessary and any treatment interventions that are indicated by those assessments.

The diagnostic phase of the program begins with a consultation between the case manager, the parents, and the child. The next step usually involves the completion of questionnaires by the child's parents and teachers aimed at determining the *general* scope and severity of the child's ADHD problem. For example, one of the most frequently used and revealing questionnaires is the Conners Teacher Rating Scale, which directs the evaluator to gauge symptoms like "restlessness" according to four degrees: "not at all," "just a little," "pretty much," and "very much."

Additional diagnostic strategies are employed in the program to arrive at a more *specific* picture of the child's ADHD problem. A pediatrician takes a detailed developmental history and conducts a lengthy physical examination; a psychologist performs one or both of the following observational studies:

■ direct observation of the child's behavior at school: in the classroom and/or on the playground;

■ direct observation of the child (via a one-way mirror) during a simulated work or play experience set up at the clinic.

To determine the extent to which learning difficulties are— or may be—involved in the case, the psychologist also administers various tests to measure the child's intelligence quotient and intellectual achievements as well as her or his abilities to control impulsivity, to concentrate, to organize her or his thoughts, and to utilize her or his memory. If psychological problems are apparent, if the family is experiencing significant conflicts, or if medication seems indicated, an extensive psychiatric evaluation is conducted. Essentially, this evaluation determines the potential or existing impact of anxiety, depression, anger, or other emotional disturbances not only on the child's ADHD itself but also on the child's ability to respond to ADHD therapy.

Specific treatment of ADHD advised by the program varies according to the case at hand. In some cases, medical management is indicated. The most common medication used to treat ADHD is Ritalin, a trade name for the stimulant methylphenidate. Alternative stimulants that may be prescribed are Dexedrine (dextroamphetamine) and Cylert (pemoline). In low dosages, these drugs enhance attention without causing an increase in motor activity.

Other ADHD cases in which medical management is indicated call for an antidepressant instead of a stimulant. The antidepressants most often prescribed for ADHD are known as tricyclic antidepressants (TCAs): namely, Tofranil or Janimine (both imipramine) and Norpramin or Pertofrane (both desipramine).

Whether or not medical management is indicated, ADHD treatment supervised by the program always consists of three integrated components: behavioral management, family counseling, and educational counseling:

■ *Behavioral management* refers to the administration of techniques by parents and teachers to change the child's ADHD-related behavior for the better. Specifically, the aim is to get the child to alter or eliminate undesirable behaviors and to adopt or increase wanted behaviors by applying a system of rewards, skills training, and environmental manipulation.

■ *Family counseling* is geared toward the promotion of healthy family interactions in general and toward the promotion of effective coping with the child's ADHD in particular. Usually it involves a series of psychotherapeutic sessions in which all members of the family participate jointly.

■ *Educational counseling* involves working with parents, teachers, and in some cases, special agencies and institutions, to make sure that the ADHD-afflicted child receives the kind of instructional, informational, and intellectual training from which she or he can best benefit.

For more information about ADHD in general, see *A Parent's Guide to Attention Deficit Disorders* by Lisa J. Bain (a Delta book, New York: Bantam Doubleday Dell Publishing, 1991). This practical book is based on the ADHD-related experience of pediatricians, psychiatrists, psychologists, neurologists, and social workers associated with PCGC, The Children's Hospital of Philadelphia, and the Children's Seashore House.

The Middle Years: Selected Terms and Concepts

acting out   indirectly expressing emotional conflicts—or "forbidden feelings"—through negative behavior. Such behavior is typically overdramatic and designed to attract attention. It may or may not be overtly self-punishing or injurious to others. For example, a child who feels rejected by a parent may "act out" that feeling by refusing to speak to that parent, constantly trying to distract the parent, or picking fights with a sibling who appears to be getting more attention.

adjustment disorder a psychological illness characterized by a child's failure to respond effectively to change or to recover effectively from a crisis.

affective disorder also known as *emotional disorder* and *mood disorder*, a specifically defined psychological illness relating to the emotions (e.g., *adjustment disorder*). Generally, such a disorder is apparent in the problematic manner in which a child physically displays her or his emotions (hence, the root "affect"). The disorder may also have a physical cause.

attachment the emotional bond between parent and child. Most often the term is used in reference to the child's bond to the mother, although attachment is a two-way street and also forms between child and father.

Attachment between child and mother is uniquely strong because of the latter's role in childbearing and early caretaking. Conditioned to seek closeness with the mother, the child may suffer emotional difficulties if deprived of maternal affections or if that affection becomes overly demanding.

attention-deficit hyperactivity disorder psychiatric disorder characterized by persistent restlessness, noisiness, inability to concentrate, poor socialization, and poor scholastic performance.

behavior modeling a therapeutic technique by means of which the child is taught or encouraged to replace negative behaviors with more positive ones. The teaching or encouraging process involves modifying the way each parent or caretaker interacts with the child so that the child learns by example or direct experience (e.g., a reward system) to behave more constructively.

bipolar disorder also known as *manic-depressive disorder*, a psychological illness characterized by extreme mood swings back and forth between depression and elation. Each mood phase lasts for an indeterminate amount of time, varying from individual to individual and from episode to episode. The disorder has a biological basis and can often be controlled by medication.

compliance the tendency to respond effectively—both in emotional and behavioral terms—to scheduling arrangements, rules, and discipline.

conduct disorder a psychological problem manifested in chronic, excessively unruly behaviors, such as stealing, running away, lying, or setting fires.

conflict resolution a therapeutic technique in which a child is assisted in alleviating or managing chronic interpersonal conflict. Often group therapy is involved, bringing together the child with the other person or persons involved in the conflict. The therapy may also, or alternatively, feature one-on-one teaching, whereby the child learns general strategies for handling interpersonal conflicts more effectively.

defense mechanism according to Sigmund Freud's terminology, a means unconsciously and automatically employed by the psyche to avoid emotional pain, such as *projection* or *repression.*

defiance more technically known as *oppositional behavior,* a term that refers to any act of a child that is intentionally designed to challenge parental authority. Common examples include saying no, refusing to perform assigned tasks, and deliberately withdrawing from meals and other prearranged family activities.

depression more technically known as *unipolar disorder,* a term that refers to a distinct psychological illness characterized by chronic apathy, hopelessness, and fatigue—physical as well as emotional.

distractibility a problematic behavior involving a limited ability to concentrate on a single activity for an appropriate amount of time. Distractibility can be a sign of underlying anxiety, or it can lead to anxiety. It can also be a symptom of attention-deficit hyperactivity disorder (see pages 124–25 in this section).

dysfunctional as opposed to *functional,* a term used to describe a personality or family unit that does not operate effectively or satisfactorily to meet day-to-day life challenges. In some cases, there is apparent effectiveness or satisfaction, but achieving it causes underlying psychological damage. In other cases, the personality or family unit is clearly having problems that pose a threat to its survival.

This term is sociological in origin and is rapidly losing currency in the field of psychology. Many therapists consider it too negative and abstract to be useful diagnostically.

eating disorder a psychological illness manifested by chronic, abnormal eating behavior. Among the most common eating disorders are "anorexia nervosa," in which the child starves her- or himself, and "bulimia," in which the child binges on food and then vomits to purge her- or himself. Eating disorders of this nature are relatively rare among children in the middle years. Instead, they tend to manifest themselves during adolescence.

Electra complex according to Sigmund Freud's philosophy, the natural psychological drive in a young girl to compete with her mother for her father's attention and affection. In other words, the father is perceived as a romantic ideal whose presence is constantly desired, while the mother is perceived as a rival, an unwanted presence.

Typically, a young girl experiences the Electra complex between the ages of three and six. Sometimes, however, its effects may linger until age eight. The counterpart of the Electra complex for young boys is the *Oedipus complex*.

emotional disorder (see *affective disorder*)

empathy the emotional and social ability of a child to respond effectively, with compassion and without self-interest, to the pains and needs of another human being. A child can demonstrate isolated instances of empathy from a very early age, especially in connection with parent, sibling, or loved one. However, the overall capacity to feel, sustain, and enact empathy is relatively limited until around ages six to eight, by which time the child has had sufficient social experience to develop such a capacity.

extroversion a generally outgoing attitude toward the world at large. First defined by Carl Jung, extroversion is also associated with a relatively strong interest in social interactions and concrete realities and a relatively weak interest in self-contained activities and abstract thought.

Extroversion is assumed to be an inborn personality trait that is neither positive nor negative in essence and that can be modified only slightly by experience or conditioning. The opposite quality is *introversion*.

functional (see *dysfunctional*)

impulsivity a child's persistent and inappropriate pattern of acting spontaneously according to personal desires without thinking of the consequences. It may be a sign of an underlying psychological problem. It may also be a symptom of attention-deficit hyperactivity disorder.

individuation   in the philosophy of Carl Jung, the long process by which a child evolves from being totally dependent on others—emotionally, intellectually, and socially—to being a separate and successful individual with a unique, self-sustaining psychological makeup.

introversion   a generally inward looking attitude toward the world at large. First defined by Carl Jung, introversion is also associated with a relatively strong interest in self-contained activities and abstract thought and a relatively mild interest in social interactions and concrete realities.

Introversion is assumed to be an inborn personality trait that is neither positive nor negative in essence and can be modified only slightly by experience or conditioning. The opposite quality is *extroversion*.

latency   according to Sigmund Freud's philosophy, the period between six and ten, when a child is relatively free from psychological upheavals having to do with sexual development. For this reason, a child during latency is considered to be more emotionally stable in general than during her or his earlier or later years.

maladaption   also known as *maladjustment*, this term refers to a child's inability to respond in a calm, effective, or successful manner either to a single life change or to the demands of life in general.

maladjustment   (see *maladaption*)

manic-depressive disorder   (see *bipolar disorder*)

medical intervention   in most cases, the use of medication (e.g., tranquilizing drugs) to alleviate the cause or symptoms of a psychological problem.

mood disorder   (see *affective disorder*)

nature versus nurture   an expression referring to the concept that some of a child's psychological traits are primarily inborn (i.e., "natural") and others are primarily acquired through upbringing (i.e., "nurturing"). Different schools of thought assign different "nature versus nurture" ratios to the development of individual psychological traits.

neurosis   as opposed to the more serious condition *psychosis*, a psychological problem that still allows the victim to maintain reasonably good contact with reality and to perform intellectually and socially in a reasonably acceptable manner.

This term does not refer to a specific illness. Therefore, it is technically not accurate to say that a child is suffering from a "neurosis." Because of this fact, the term is rapidly being replaced by the expression "neurotic process" (e.g., "If treatment is not applied, this child's emotional problem could trigger a neurotic process").

obsessive behavior a pattern of applying excessively intense and perhaps ritualized concentration to the performance of a specific task (e.g., hand washing). Often the child's preoccupation with a particular task appears to be fanatical—a desperate quest for certainty or perfection. If the behavior persists over an extended period of time, it could be a sign of an underlying psychological problem.

Oedipus complex according to Sigmund Freud's philosophy, the natural psychological drive in a young boy to compete with his father for his mother's attention and affection. In other words, the mother is perceived as a romantic ideal whose presence is constantly desired, while the father is perceived as a rival and unwanted presence.

Typically, a young boy experiences the Oedipus complex between the ages of three and six. Sometimes, however, its effects may linger until age eight. The counterpart of the Oedipus complex for young girls is called the *Electra complex*.

oppositional behavior (see *defiance*)

other-directed behavior individual actions that are oriented toward other people: for example, seeking their attention, initiating and responding to interactions, expressing hostility. Therapists often explore whether a child has a healthy, age-appropriate balance of other-directed behavior and its opposite, *self-directed behavior*.

overanxious disorder a psychological problem manifesting itself in chronic, generalized, and often irrational feelings of fear, apprehension, and misgiving. There may also be physical symptoms, such as frequent headaches and stomachaches.

overcorrection a negative effect of the parent-child relationship in which the discipline or punishment imposed on a child's conduct—or the child's "reforming" response to discipline or punishment—exceeds appropriate limits.

pathology (see *psychopathology*)

phobia   an excessive and persistent fear of particular people, things, or situations. (Precise targets vary from individual to individual.) Phobias are fairly common among children in the middle years. Most often they are transitory and not indicative of any serious psychological problem.

projection   an unconscious, self-protecting measure in which a child denies negative, forbidden, or unpleasant feelings and instead attributes them to someone else. In most cases, the person upon whom the child projects such negative feelings is the trigger for them. For example, a child who is angry at Mother may unconsciously reclaim her or his innocence by believing instead that Mother is angry with her or him.

psychoanalysis   as opposed to the broader term *psychotherapy*, a mode of diagnosing and treating a child's psychological problems through one-on-one therapist-patient dialogue. There are many different schools of psychoanalysis, each based on a particular philosophy regarding how the psyche functions.

Because of its reliance on verbal and cognitive skills, psychoanalysis is more often applied to adolescents and adults than to children in their middle years. The latter group is more often diagnosed and treated by means of therapies in which the whole family participates or in which the object is *behavior modeling* rather than intellectual understanding.

psychopathology   the study of mental illnesses. The term *pathology* refers to a disease or a disorder, as opposed to a less severe problem.

psychosis   as opposed to the less serious condition *neurosis*, a psychological problem that often or continuously prevents the victim from maintaining reasonably good contact with reality or performing intellectually and socially in a reasonably acceptable manner.

A particular psychotic disorder may be either psychological or biological in origin or both. Among the distinctive indicators that an emotional problem is psychotic rather than neurotic are the presence of delusions (irrational beliefs) or hallucinations (distorted perceptions).

psychotherapy   a professional method of treating emotional problems and *affective disorders*. Psychotherapy can take a number of different forms, such as *psychoanalysis*, or varying therapies designed to provide appropriate *behavior modeling*.

repression a means of emotional self-protection in which traumatic or unpleasant thoughts or memories are automatically relegated to the unconscious mind and forgotten by the conscious mind.

resilience a child's ability to adapt effectively to change or recover effectively from a crisis. The more resilient a child's emotional nature is, the psychologically healthier she or he is.

resistance in the context of psychotherapy, a child's conscious or unconscious refusal to cooperate with the therapist or the therapy.

self-directed behavior individual actions that are oriented around the self: for example, solitary play or self-punishment. Therapists often explore whether a child has a healthy, age-appropriate balance of self-directed behavior and its opposite, *other-directed behavior.*

unipolar disorder (see *depression*)

withdrawal a child's willful separation, emotionally or physically, from an event or person that is somehow distressing. Long-term withdrawal, or an ever-widening pattern of withdrawal, can be a sign of an underlying psychological problem.

Appendix

Organizations to Contact

If you believe your child is having serious problems dealing with her or his emotions or behavior, it's a good idea to get a professional evaluation of your child's emotional health and, possibly, professional help for your child. These services should be provided by a well-qualified child psychiatrist, child psychologist, or social worker whom both you and your child like and trust.

To find the professional that's right for your situation, first consult friends and relatives who have had experience with such services, your pediatrician, and your child's school counselor. Also try local organizations, such as medical societies, psychiatric societies, and city, county, and state mental-health associations.

If you are unable to get satisfactory references or locate an acceptable professional using these sources, or if you'd like more background information on the subject and practice of psychotherapy for children, try contacting any of the following organizations for assistance:

American Academy of Child and Adolescent Psychiatry
3615 Wisconsin Avenue, NW
Washington, DC 20016
(800) 222-7636

■ professional society for degreed physicians who have completed an additional five years of residency in child and adolescent psychiatry

■ forty-three regional groups in the United States, equipped to provide information (including consumer guidance on insurance benefits covering child and adolescent psychiatry) and referrals

American Academy of Community Psychiatrists
P.O. Box 5372
Arlington, VA 22205
(703) 237-0823

■ professional society for psychiatrists and psychiatry residents practicing in community mental-health centers or similar programs that provide care regardless of their client's ability to pay

■ seven regional groups in the United States that are equipped to inform the public about a community psychiatrist's training and role and about how to obtain services

American Association of Psychiatric Services for Children
1200-C Scottsville Road, Suite 225
Rochester, NY 14624
(716) 235-6910

■ accrediting service and information clearinghouse for clinics and other institutions offering psychiatric services for children

■ equipped to provide information and referrals

National Association of Social Workers
7981 Eastern Avenue
Silver Spring, MD 20910
(800) 638-8799

■ professional society for people who hold a minimum of a baccalaureate degree in social work (B.S.W.)

■ fifty-five state, district, and protectorate groups that are equipped to inform the public about the services provided by social workers and how to obtain them

American Association for Marriage and Family Therapy
1717 K Street, NW #407
Washington, DC 20006
(202) 429-1825

■ professional society for marriage and family therapists

■ maintains thirty-nine training centers throughout United States that are equipped to provide information and referrals

Psychology Society
100 Beekman Street
New York, NY 10038
(212) 285-1872

■ professional society for psychologists who have a doctorate and are certified/licensed in the state where they practice

■ equipped to provide information and referrals

National Association for the Advancement of Psychoanalysis
and the American Boards for Accreditation and Certification
80 Eighth Avenue, Suite 1210
New York, NY 10011
(212) 741-0515

■ professional society for psychoanalysts that sets standards for training, accredits institutions, certifies individual practitioners, and evaluates institutions and practitioners

■ equipped to offer information and referrals (publishes an annual directory, *National Registry of Psychoanalysts*, with geographic index: $15)

Council for the National Register of Health Service Providers
in Psychology
1730 Rhode Island Avenue, NW, Suite 1200
Washington, DC 20036
(202) 833-2377

■ registry for psychologists who are licensed or certified by a state board of examiners of psychology and who have met additional council criteria as health service providers in psychology

■ equipped to provide referrals

National Council of Community Mental Health Centers
12300 Twinbrook Parkway
Rockville, MD 20852

■ membership organization of community mental-health centers

■ not equipped to provide referrals by telephone but publishes a bi-annual *National Registry*, which lists centers by geographic area

Federation of Families for Children's Mental Health
1021 Prince Street
Alexandria, VA 22314
(703) 684-7710

■ organization for parents looking for support and advocacy groups

■ equipped to provide contacts

Index